# The Delicious Slow Cooker Cookbook for Two People 2025:

## 2000 Days of Super Easy, Budget-Friendly, No-Waste, & Time-Saving, Portioned Crockpot Recipes. For Beginners and Advanced Cooks.
## Bonus Inside.

Emmanuel C.A

# Copyright

© 2025 by Emmanuel C.A.

All rights reserved. No part of this publication may be reproduced, distributed, or transmitted in any form or by any means, including photocopying, recording, or other electronic or mechanical methods, without the prior written permission of the author, except in the case of brief quotations embodied in critical reviews and certain other noncommercial uses permitted by copyright law.

Disclaimer

The contents of this book are provided for general informational purposes only. The author and publisher make no representations or warranties regarding the accuracy, completeness, or suitability of the information contained herein. The material is offered because it does not constitute professional advice.
Readers are encouraged to independently verify any information provided and seek professional advice tailored to their circumstances. The author and publisher shall not be held responsible for any errors or omissions, or any consequences arising from the use of the information presented in this book.

By reading this book, you acknowledge and agree to the terms of this disclaimer.

# Table of Contents

# INTRODUCTION

## The Power of Slow Cooking for Two

Cooking should be enjoyable, not overwhelming. Slow cooking is one of the most effortless ways to prepare flavorful, comforting meals with minimal effort. Whether you're a busy professional, a student, or simply someone who enjoys home-cooked meals without the stress, a slow cooker is your best kitchen companion.

This cookbook is specifically designed for those cooking for two—eliminating excessive leftovers while ensuring every meal is perfectly portioned. With slow cooking, flavors deepen over time, ingredients tenderize beautifully, and meals become effortlessly delicious.

## Why Slow Cooking?

Convenience: Prep your ingredients, set your slow cooker, and go about your day while it does the work for you. No standing over the stove or constant stirring.

Enhanced Flavor: Slow cooking allows ingredients to meld together, creating rich, deep flavors that you simply can't achieve with quick cooking methods.

Less Waste, More Savings: Cooking for two means no excess food sitting in the fridge, leading to less waste and more mindful grocery shopping.

Hands-Off Cooking: With just a few minutes of prep, you can enjoy homemade meals without the stress of last-minute cooking.

Tender, Delicious Meals: Slow cooking ensures that every bite of soups, stews, curries, and casseroles is infused with flavor and cooked to perfection.

What's Inside This Cookbook?

A collection of slow cooker recipes crafted for two servings—no more, no less.

Various dishes, from hearty breakfasts and cozy soups to satisfying mains and indulgent desserts.

Time-saving tips to get the most out of your slow cooker.

A dedicated section on handling leftovers and making the most of extra portions.

Whether you're new to slow cooking or a seasoned home cook, this book will help you create simple, satisfying meals without the guesswork. Get ready to embrace the ease, flavor, and joy of slow cooking—one perfectly portioned meal at a time!

Simple Techniques, Extraordinary Results

Slow cooking is one of the most effortless ways to prepare flavorful, satisfying meals, but mastering a few key techniques can take your dishes from good to exceptional. With a little attention to detail, you can create slow-cooked meals that are rich in depth, perfectly textured, and bursting with flavor. Whether you are new to slow cooking or a seasoned home cook looking to refine your skills, these simple yet powerful strategies will help you make the most of your slow cooker.

1. Layer Ingredients for Even Cooking: One of the most important techniques in slow cooking is proper ingredient layering. Since heat is primarily distributed from the bottom of the slow cooker, placing ingredients in the right order ensures even cooking and prevents overcooked or undercooked components.

Root vegetables first: Dense vegetables like potatoes, carrots, and parsnips take the longest to cook, so they should be placed at the bottom where they receive the most heat.

Proteins and grains in the middle: Chicken, beef, lentils, and grains should be added next, nestled among the vegetables.

Delicate ingredients last: Tender vegetables, fresh herbs, dairy, and quick-cooking ingredients should be added toward the end of cooking to preserve their flavor and texture.

By following this layering method, you'll ensure that all ingredients cook at the right pace, resulting in perfectly balanced meals.

2. Brown Proteins for Richer Flavor: While slow cookers do an excellent job of tenderizing meat and developing deep flavors over time, taking a few extra minutes to brown your proteins before adding them to the slow cooker can significantly enhance the taste and texture of your dish.

Caramelization: Searing meat at high heat creates a flavorful crust, locking in juices and adding complexity to the dish.

Aromatic depth: Sautéing onions, garlic, and spices before slow cooking releases their essential oils, intensifying their fragrance and taste.

For best results, heat a skillet over medium-high heat, add a small amount of oil, and sear meats or aromatics until golden brown before transferring them to the slow cooker. This small step makes a world of difference in the final dish.

3. Use the Right Amount of Liquid: Unlike traditional stovetop or oven cooking, slow cookers retain moisture and require less liquid than other cooking methods. Too much liquid can result in a watery, diluted dish, while too little can cause ingredients to dry out or burn.
Start with less liquid: Many ingredients, such as vegetables and meats, release moisture as they cook. If a dish seems dry, you can always add more liquid later.
Consider evaporation: If you prefer a thicker sauce, remove the lid during the last 30 minutes of cooking to allow some liquid to evaporate.

Balance flavors: Broths, stocks, and canned tomatoes contribute more depth than plain water, so opt for these flavorful liquids whenever possible.
By keeping liquid levels in check, you'll achieve a perfectly balanced consistency in every meal.

4. Avoid Lifting the Lid Too Often: One of the most common mistakes in slow cooking is constantly opening the lid to check on progress. Every time the lid is lifted, heat escapes, and the internal temperature drops, increasing the overall cooking time.

Each lift adds 20-30 minutes: Heat loss slows the cooking process, meaning your meal could take much longer than expected.
Minimal stirring required: Unlike stovetop cooking, slow-cooked dishes do not need frequent stirring. Let the slow cooker do its job.
For best results, trust the process and resist the urge to peek too often.

5. Adjust Cooking Times Based on Your Slow Cooker: Not all slow cookers operate at the same temperature. Some models run hotter than others, which can affect cooking times. Understanding how your specific slow cooker behaves will help you achieve consistent results.
Newer models tend to cook faster: If you find that dishes finish cooking sooner than expected, reduce the cooking time slightly.

Older models may require extra time: If your slow cooker seems to take longer than recipes suggest, adjust accordingly.

Test doneness with a fork: If meats are easily shredded and vegetables are fork-tender, the dish is ready.

By getting to know your slow cooker's quirks, you'll be able to tailor cooking times for perfect results every time.

6. Season Wisely for Maximum Flavor: Slow cooking mellows the intensity of many spices and seasonings, so it's important to adjust when and how you add flavors.

Layer seasonings throughout the cooking process: Adding bold spices at the beginning builds a strong base, while delicate seasonings (like fresh herbs or citrus juice) should be added at the end for a bright finish.

Salt absorbs over time: If a dish tastes bland, wait until the end of cooking before adjusting the seasoning—flavors become more concentrated as moisture reduces.

Boost umami: Ingredients like tomato paste, soy sauce, Worcestershire sauce, or Parmesan rinds can add depth and complexity to slow-cooked meals.

With proper seasoning, your dishes will have a well-rounded, robust taste that doesn't fade over long cooking hours.

7. Thicken Sauces and Soups the Right Way: Since slow cookers trap moisture, sauces, and soups can sometimes end up thinner than desired. If you want a thicker consistency:

Remove the lid: Letting the dish cook uncovered for the last 30-45 minutes allows excess moisture to evaporate.

Use a thickening agent: Stir in a slurry of cornstarch (1 tablespoon mixed with 1 tablespoon water) or a flour-based roux for a silkier texture.

Mash ingredients: For stews and soups, mashing some of the cooked vegetables can naturally thicken the broth.

By controlling moisture levels, you can create luxurious, restaurant-quality textures at home.

8. Make the Recipes Your Own: One of the best aspects of slow cooking is its flexibility. Every recipe in this book has been carefully crafted for ideal flavors and portion sizes, but you can easily customize them to suit your preferences.

Adjust spice levels: If you enjoy bold flavors, increase spices and herbs. If you prefer milder dishes, scale them back.

Swap ingredients: Not a fan of a particular vegetable or protein? Substitute with a similar ingredient that you love.

Make extra for future meals: If you have a larger slow cooker, consider doubling a recipe and freezing leftovers for later.

Slow cooking is about convenience, creativity, and comfort. Feel free to experiment and make each dish uniquely yours.

By mastering these simple yet powerful techniques, you'll unlock the full potential of slow cooking. With minimal effort and a little planning, you can create extraordinary meals that are rich in flavor, perfectly cooked, and deeply satisfying. Whether you're preparing a cozy dinner for two or experimenting with new flavors, these expert tips will ensure that every dish is a success.

Slow cooking isn't just about making meals—it's about making mealtime easier, more enjoyable, and incredibly delicious.

**Introduction to Recipes**

Within this cookbook, you will discover a collection of carefully crafted recipes tailored for two servings. Designed with simplicity in mind, each recipe is easy to follow, using common ingredients and minimal preparation time. Whether you're a beginner or an experienced cook, the recipes in this book will empower you to create delicious, satisfying meals with minimal effort.

Every dish is specifically portioned for two, ensuring that you can enjoy flavorful meals without worrying about excessive leftovers. These recipes offer an opportunity to indulge in diverse and exciting flavors, all while keeping the process straightforward and approachable.

The beauty of slow cooking lies in its ability to transform humble ingredients into something extraordinary, and that is exactly what you will experience with each dish. The slow cooker does all the hard work for you, melding ingredients together and enhancing flavors over time. You'll find that with a little patience, you'll be rewarded with rich, comforting meals.

As you progress through the recipes, you'll notice that many of them feature familiar, easy-to-find ingredients, yet they deliver bold and diverse flavor profiles. From hearty soups to creamy stews, and savory curries to delectable sides, each recipe is designed to make the most of your slow cooker's potential.

By focusing on smaller portions, these recipes are ideal for busy individuals or couples who want to enjoy home-cooked meals without the hassle of preparing excessive quantities. Each recipe also provides ample room for experimentation—feel free to tweak ingredients or adjust the spice levels to match your personal preferences.

# CHAPTER ONE: BREAKFAST RECIPES

## Slow Cooker Dulce de Leche (Caramel)

Preparation Time: 5 minutes
Cooking Time: 6–8 hours on low
Yield: About 4–6 tablespoons (small batch), suitable for two light servings

### Ingredients
- 1/4 (3.5 ounces) can of sweetened condensed milk

### Instructions
1. Pour the 3.5 ounces of sweetened condensed milk into a small heatproof glass jar or canning jar with a tight-fitting lid.
2. Place the jar on its side in the slow cooker.
3. Add enough hot water to the slow cooker to submerge the jar completely, ensuring the water level is at least 1 inch above the jar.
4. Cover the slow cooker and cook on low for 6–8 hours. Cook for 6 hours for a lighter caramel or 8 hours for a darker, richer caramel.
5. Carefully remove the jar from the slow cooker using tongs (it will be very hot). Allow the jar to cool completely before opening. Do not open the jar while it is hot, as this can be dangerous.
6. Once cooled, open the jar and stir the dulce de leche until smooth.

**Storage:** If there are any leftovers, transfer them to an airtight container and refrigerate. Use within three days for the best quality.

**Notes:** For Larger Portions: If you'd like a slightly larger batch for generous servings or leftovers, double the recipe by using 7 ounces (1/2 can) of sweetened condensed milk. Follow the same steps, and you'll yield about 3/4 cup of dulce de leche.
Leftover Ideas: Any leftovers can be used as a topping for ice cream, pancakes, waffles, or fruit, or as a filling for pastries.
Storage for Larger Batches: A sealed jar of dulce de leche can last in the refrigerator for 1–2 weeks.

**Safety Tip:** Ensure the jar remains fully submerged in water throughout cooking. If water levels drop due to evaporation, add more hot water to maintain proper coverage.

---

# Slow Cooker Chocolate Peanut Butter Fudge

Portioning: Yields a small batch, ideal for two servings. Preparation Time: 10 minutes Cooking Time: 1.5–2 hours on low, plus chilling time

## Ingredients

- 1/2 cup (100g) semi-sweet chocolate chips
- 1/4 cup (62g) creamy peanut butter
- 2 tablespoons (28g) sweetened condensed milk
- 1/8 teaspoon vanilla extract
- A small pinch of salt

## Instructions

1. Line a small dish or container (approximately 3x3 inches) with parchment paper, leaving extra paper hanging over the edges for easy removal.
2. In the slow cooker, combine the chocolate chips, peanut butter, sweetened condensed milk, and salt.
3. Cover and cook on low for 1.5–2 hours, stirring every 30 minutes until the chocolate is melted and the mixture is smooth.
4. Stir in the vanilla extract.
5. Pour the mixture into the prepared dish and spread it evenly.
6. Cover and refrigerate for at least 2 hours, or until completely firm.
7. Use the parchment paper overhang to lift the fudge out of the dish. Slice into small squares and enjoy.

**Storage:** Store any leftover fudge in an airtight container in the refrigerator for up to one week.

**Safety Note:** Ensure the slow cooker is set to low heat to prevent scorching. Stirring every 30 minutes helps maintain an even consistency.

## Slow Cooker Berry Cobbler for Two

Portioning: Two satisfying servings.
Prep Time: 15 minutes
Cook Time: 2–2.5 hours on low

### Ingredients
- 1.5 cups mixed berries (fresh or frozen – if frozen, do not thaw)
- 1 tablespoon granulated sugar (or more, to taste)
- 1/2 tablespoon cornstarch
- 1/2 tablespoon lemon juice

### For the topping:
- 1/4 cup all-purpose flour
- 2 tablespoons granulated sugar
- 1/2 teaspoon baking powder
- A pinch of salt
- 2 tablespoons milk
- 1 tablespoon melted butter

### Instructions:
1. Prepare the Berry Filling: In a small bowl, toss the berries with sugar, cornstarch, and lemon juice until evenly coated.
2. Set Up the Slow Cooker: Transfer the berry mixture to a small (about 1/2- to 1-quart) oven-safe dish that fits in your slow cooker.
3. Mix the Topping: In a separate bowl, whisk together the flour, sugar, baking powder, and salt. Add the milk and melted butter, stirring until just combined.
4. Assemble the Cobbler: Drop spoonfuls of the batter over the berries, leaving some gaps to let the berries bubble through.
5. Cook the Cobbler: Place the dish in the slow cooker, cover, and cook on low for 2–2.5 hours, or until the topping is set, lightly golden, and the berries are bubbling.

Storage and Reheating Instructions (if needed):

**Storage:** If there is a small leftover portion, let it cool completely, transfer it to an airtight container, and refrigerate. Use within 1–2 days.

**Reheating:** Place the leftover portion back into the slow cooker. Add a small splash of water to the dish (to prevent drying out), cover, and reheat on low for about 30 minutes, or until warmed through.

---

## Slow Cooker Rice Pudding

Portioning: Serves two generous portions.
Prep Time: 5 minutes
Cook Time: 2–3 hours on low

### Ingredients

- 1/4 cup uncooked long-grain rice (do not use instant rice)
- 1 1/2 cups whole milk (for a creamy texture)
- 1/4 cup granulated sugar (adjust to your preference)
- 1/4 teaspoon ground cinnamon
- 1/4 teaspoon vanilla extract
- A pinch of salt
- Optional: 1/4 cup raisins or other dried fruit (add in the last 30 minutes of cooking)

### Instructions:

1. In the slow cooker, combine the rice, milk, sugar, cinnamon, and salt.
2. Cover the slow cooker and cook on low for 2–3 hours, stirring occasionally during the last hour to prevent sticking. The rice should be tender, and the pudding should be creamy.
3. If you're using raisins or dried fruit, stir them in during the last 30 minutes of cooking.
4. Once the rice pudding is ready, mix in the vanilla extract.
5. Serve the rice pudding warm or chilled.

# Slow Cooker Pineapple Upside-Down Cake

Portioning: Makes two generous slices.
Prep Time: 15 minutes
Cook Time: 2–2.5 hours on low

## Ingredients

- For the topping:
- 2 tablespoons melted butter
- 2 tablespoons packed brown sugar
- 4 pineapple rings (canned, drained)
- 4 maraschino cherries (optional)

## For the cake:

- 1/2 cup all-purpose flour
- 1/4 cup granulated sugar
- 1/2 teaspoon baking powder
- 1/4 teaspoon salt
- 1/4 cup milk
- 1 tablespoon melted butter
- 1/2 teaspoon vanilla extract

## Instructions

1. Lightly grease a small (about 6-inch) oven-safe dish that will fit into your slow cooker.

2. Pour the melted butter into the dish and evenly sprinkle the brown sugar on top. Arrange the pineapple rings and cherries (if using) on top of the brown sugar.

3. In a medium-sized bowl, whisk together the flour, granulated sugar, baking powder, and salt.

4. In a separate small bowl, mix the milk, melted butter, and vanilla extract.

5. Add the wet ingredients to the dry ingredients and stir until just combined. Avoid overmixing.

6. Pour the batter evenly over the pineapple in the dish.

7. Place the dish in the slow cooker, cover it, and cook on low for 2–2.5 hours, or until a toothpick inserted in the center comes out clean.

8. Carefully remove the dish from the slow cooker. Let it cool for about 10 minutes before flipping it onto a serving plate.

## Slow Cooker Overnight Apple Cinnamon Steel-Cut Oats

Portioning: Makes two generous servings.
Prep Time: 10 minutes
Cook Time: 6–8 hours on low (or overnight)

### Ingredients

- 1/2 cup steel-cut oats
- 2 cups unsweetened almond milk (or any milk of your choice)
- 1 medium apple, cored and diced
- 1 tablespoon maple syrup (or honey, or adjust to taste)
- 1 teaspoon ground cinnamon
- 1/4 teaspoon ground nutmeg
- A pinch of salt
- Optional toppings: chopped nuts, peanut butter drizzle, or a sprinkle of cinnamon

### Instructions:

1. Add all the ingredients to a 2-quart slow cooker.
2. Stir everything together until well combined.
3. Cover the slow cooker and cook on low for 6–8 hours, or overnight. The oats should be creamy, and most of the liquid will be absorbed. If there's any extra liquid, simply stir it in the serving.
4. Stir the oats again before serving. Add any optional toppings as desired.

# Slow Cooker Banana Bread Oatmeal

Portioning: Makes two satisfying servings.
Prep Time: 10 minutes
Cook Time: 2–3 hours on low

## Ingredients

- 1 cup rolled oats (not instant)
- 2 cups unsweetened almond milk
- 1 ripe banana, mashed
- 1 tablespoon packed brown sugar (adjust to taste)
- 1/2 teaspoon ground cinnamon
- 1/4 teaspoon ground nutmeg
- 1/4 teaspoon vanilla extract
- A pinch of salt
- Optional toppings: sliced bananas, chopped walnuts

## Instructions

1. Add all the ingredients into a 2-quart slow cooker.
2. Stir to combine everything thoroughly.
3. Cover the slow cooker and cook on low for 2–3 hours, or until the oats are soft and creamy. Stir occasionally during the last hour to prevent sticking.
4. Serve warm with your choice of toppings.

## Slow Cooker Pumpkin Pie Oatmeal

Portioning: Makes two comforting servings.
Prep Time: 10 minutes
Cook Time: 2–3 hours on low

### Ingredients

- 1 cup rolled oats
- 2 cups unsweetened almond milk
- 1/2 cup pumpkin puree (not pumpkin pie filling)
- 2 tablespoons maple syrup (or adjust to taste)
- 1 teaspoon pumpkin pie spice
- 1/4 teaspoon vanilla extract
- Pinch of salt
- Optional toppings: chopped pecans, Greek yogurt

### Instructions

1. Add all the ingredients into a 2-quart slow cooker.
2. Stir everything together until well mixed.
3. Cover and cook on low for 2–3 hours, or until the oats become creamy.
4. Serve while warm, adding any desired toppings. If necessary, adjust the sweetness with extra maple syrup after cooking.

# Slow Cooker Mixed Berry Compote with Greek Yogurt

Portioning: Makes two servings with Greek yogurt.
Prep Time: 5 minutes
Cook Time: 2-3 hours on low

## Ingredients

- 2 cups mixed berries (fresh or frozen)
- 1 tablespoon honey or maple syrup (optional, or to taste)
- 1 tablespoon lemon juice
- 1/2 teaspoon vanilla extract
- To serve: 1 cup nonfat plain Greek yogurt (1/2 cup per serving)

## Instructions

1. Place the berries, honey/maple syrup (if using), lemon juice, and vanilla extract in the slow cooker.

2. Cover and cook on low for 2-3 hours, or until the berries have softened and released their juices.

3. Serve warm or chilled, spooning the compote over 1/2 cup of Greek yogurt per serving.

## Slow Cooker Breakfast Quinoa with Fruit and Nuts

Portioning: Makes hearty servings.
Prep Time: 10 minutes
Cook Time: 2-3 hours on low

### Ingredients

- 1/2 cup quinoa, rinsed
- 1 1/2 cups unsweetened almond milk
- 1/2 teaspoon ground cinnamon
- Pinch of salt
- Toppings: 1 cup chopped fresh fruit (such as berries, banana, or apple), 2 chopped nuts, 1 tablespoon honey or maple syrup (optional)

### Instructions

1. Rinse the quinoa using a fine-mesh sieve to remove any excess starch.
2. Add the rinsed quinoa, almond milk, cinnamon, and salt to the slow cooker.
3. Cover and cook on low for 2-3 hours, or until the quinoa is tender and the liquid has been absorbed
4. Serve each portion with 1/2 cup of chopped fruit, 1 tablespoon of nuts, and a drizzle of honey or maple syrup, if desired.

# CHAPTER TWO: LUNCH RECIPES

## Slow Cooker Lentil Soup with Sweet Potato and Coconut Milk

Serving Size: Two generous bowls
Prep Time: 15 minutes
Cook Time: 4-6 hours on low

## Ingredients
- 1 cup red lentils, rinsed
- 1 medium sweet potato, peeled and diced
- 1 (14-ounce) can light coconut milk
- 4 cups vegetable broth
- 1 onion, chopped
- 2 garlic cloves, minced
- 1 teaspoon ground cumin
- 1/2 teaspoon ground coriander
- 1/4 teaspoon turmeric
- A pinch of red pepper flakes (optional)
- Salt and pepper to taste

## Instructions
1. Add all ingredients to the slow cooker.
2. Stir to combine.
3. Cover the slow cooker and cook on low for 4-6 hours, or until the lentils are soft and the sweet potato is tender.
4. Serve

# Slow Cooker Vegetarian Chili with Apples and Butternut Squash

Portioning: Two hearty bowls of chili.
Prep Time: 20 minutes
Cook Time: 4-6 hours on low

## Ingredients

- 1/2 medium butternut squash, peeled, seeded, and diced
- 1 medium apple, cored and chopped
- 1/2 (15-ounce) can of black beans, rinsed and drained
- 1/2 (15-ounce) can of kidney beans, rinsed and drained
- 1 (14-ounce) can of crushed tomatoes (half the usual amount)
- 1/2 onion, chopped
- 1 clove garlic, minced
- 1 tablespoon chili powder
- 1/2 teaspoon cumin
- 1/4 teaspoon smoked paprika
- 1/8 teaspoon cinnamon
- Salt and pepper to taste

## Instructions

1. Combine all ingredients in the slow cooker.
2. Cover and cook on low for 4-6 hours, or until the butternut squash is tender.
3. Stir well before serving.

# Slow Cooker Pineapple Chicken with Coconut Rice

Servings: Makes just enough for two people.
Prep Time: 10 minutes
Cook Time: 3-4 hours on low

## Ingredients
- **For the chicken:**
  - 8 oz boneless, skinless chicken breast or thighs (1 medium piece)
  - 1 cup crushed pineapple, including juice
  - 1/4 cup coconut milk (light or full-fat)
  - 2 tablespoons low-sodium soy sauce or tamari
  - 1/4 red bell pepper, diced
  - 1/4 green bell pepper, diced
  - 1/4 onion, diced
- **For the rice:**
  - 1/2 cup uncooked white or brown rice
  - 1 cup water or broth

## Instructions
1. Prepare the base: Add the chicken to the bottom of your slow cooker. Spread the diced red and green bell peppers and onion over the chicken.
2. Mix the sauce: In a small mixing bowl, combine the crushed pineapple with its juice, coconut milk, and soy sauce. Stir until blended, then pour the mixture evenly over the chicken and vegetables in the slow cooker.
3. Cook the chicken: Cover the slow cooker and cook on low for 3-4 hours, or until the chicken is fully cooked and tender.
4. Make the rice: While the chicken cooks, prepare the rice. Add 1/2 cup of rice and 1 cup of water or broth to a small pot. Bring it to a boil, then reduce the heat, cover, and simmer for 15-20 minutes, or until the liquid is absorbed and the rice is fluffy.
5. Finish and serve: Once the chicken is cooked, shred it gently using two forks and stir it into the sauce. Divide the cooked rice into two bowls or plates. Spoon the chicken, sauce, and vegetables over the rice. Serve warm.

# Slow Cooker Maple-Glazed Chicken with Apples and Onions

Servings: Perfectly portioned for two.
Preparation Time: 10 minutes
Cooking Time: 3-4 hours on low

## Ingredients

- 3/4 lb boneless, skinless chicken thighs (1-2 small pieces)
- 1 medium apple, sliced (e.g., Honeycrisp or Gala)
- 1/2 large onion, thinly sliced
- 3 tablespoons pure maple syrup
- 1 tablespoon apple cider vinegar
- 2 teaspoons Dijon mustard
- 1/4 teaspoon dried thyme
- Salt and black pepper, to taste

## Instructions

1. Layer the base: Arrange the sliced onions in a small slow cooker (2-3 quarts). Add the sliced apples on top of the onions.

2. Add the chicken: Place the chicken thighs on top of the apples and onions.

3. Mix the sauce: In a small bowl, whisk together the maple syrup, apple cider vinegar, Dijon mustard, thyme, salt, and black pepper until well combined.

4. Pour the sauce: Drizzle the prepared sauce evenly over the chicken, apples, and onions.

5. Cook slowly: Cover the slow cooker with its lid and set it to low. Let the chicken cook for 3-4 hours, or until tender and its internal temperature reaches 165°F (74°C).

6. Shred the chicken: Once done, carefully remove the chicken, shred it using two forks, and return it to the slow cooker. Stir well to coat the shredded chicken in the flavorful sauce.

7. Serve and enjoy: Plate the chicken with apples and onions, along with a drizzle of the sauce. Pair it with a salad, roasted vegetables, or your favorite bread for a complete meal.

---

# Slow Cooker Turkey Meatballs with Cranberry Sauce

Servings: Two portions
Prep Time: 20 minutes
Cook Time: 3-4 hours on low

## Ingredients
- For the meatballs:
- 1/2 lb ground turkey (93% lean or leaner recommended)
- 2 tablespoons plain breadcrumbs (whole wheat if preferred)
- 1 small egg, lightly beaten
- 2 tablespoons onion, finely chopped
- 1 small garlic clove, minced
- 1/2 tablespoon fresh parsley, chopped
- 1/4 teaspoon dried Italian seasoning
- Salt and pepper, to taste

## For the sauce:
- 1/2 cup whole berry cranberry sauce (not jelly)
- 2 tablespoons orange juice (fresh or from concentrate)
- 1 teaspoon Dijon mustard

## Instructions
1. 1. Prepare the meatballs: In a medium bowl, combine the ground turkey, breadcrumbs, egg, onion, garlic, parsley, Italian seasoning, salt, and pepper.
2. Mix gently using your hands until just combined to avoid tough meatballs.
3. 2. Shape the meatballs: Roll the mixture into small, even-sized meatballs, approximately 1 inch in diameter.
4. 3. Prepare the sauce: In the slow cooker, whisk together the cranberry sauce, orange juice, and Dijon mustard until smooth.
   4. Cook the meatballs: Place the meatballs in the slow cooker, arranging them in a single layer if possible to ensure even cooking.
   Cover and cook on low for 3-4 hours, or until the meatballs reach an internal temperature of 165°F (74°C).

5. Serve: Once cooked, serve the meatballs hot with the cranberry sauce. This dish pairs well with steamed vegetables or a small side salad.

---

## Slow Cooker Honey Garlic Chicken with Sweet Potatoes

Preparation Time: 15 minutes
Cooking Time: 4 hours on low
Servings: 2

### Ingredients:
- 2 boneless, skinless chicken breasts
- 1 medium sweet potato, peeled and diced
- 2 cloves garlic, minced
- 2 tablespoons honey
- 1 tablespoon low-sodium soy sauce
- 1 tablespoon olive oil
- ½ teaspoon dried thyme
- Salt and pepper to taste
- Fresh parsley for garnish (optional)

### Instructions:
1. In a small bowl, whisk together honey, soy sauce, olive oil, minced garlic, dried thyme, salt, and pepper.
2. Place the diced sweet potatoes at the bottom of the slow cooker.
3. Lay the chicken breasts on top of the sweet potatoes.
4. Pour the honey-garlic mixture over the chicken and sweet potatoes, ensuring everything is well-coated.
5. Cover and cook on low for 4 hours, or until the chicken is cooked through and the sweet potatoes are tender.
6. Serve hot, garnished with fresh parsley if desired.

# Slow Cooker Maple-Glazed Salmon with Quinoa

Preparation Time: 10 minutes
Cooking Time: 2 hours on low
Servings: 2

## Ingredients:
- 2 salmon fillets (about 6 ounces each)
- ¼ cup pure maple syrup
- 1 tablespoon Dijon mustard
- 1 tablespoon low-sodium soy sauce
- 1 clove garlic, minced
- 1 cup quinoa, rinsed
- 2 cups low-sodium vegetable broth
- Salt and pepper to taste
- Fresh dill for garnish (optional)

## Instructions:
1. In a small bowl, whisk together maple syrup, Dijon mustard, soy sauce, and minced garlic.
2. Place the salmon fillets in a shallow dish and pour half of the maple mixture over them. Let them marinate for about 10 minutes.
3. In the meantime, add rinsed quinoa and vegetable broth to the slow cooker. Season with a pinch of salt and pepper.
4. Place a piece of parchment paper or aluminum foil over the quinoa mixture, then lay the marinated salmon fillets on top. Drizzle with the remaining maple mixture.
5. Cover and cook on low for 2 hours, or until the salmon flakes easily with a fork and the quinoa is cooked.
6. Serve the salmon over the quinoa, garnished with fresh dill if desired.

# Slow Cooker Coconut Curry Lentil Soup

Preparation Time: 15 minutes
Cooking Time: 4 hours on low
Servings: 2

## Ingredients:
- 1 cup red lentils, rinsed
- 1 small onion, finely chopped
- 2 cloves garlic, minced
- 1 medium carrot, diced
- 1 small sweet potato, peeled and diced
- 1 tablespoon curry powder
- ½ teaspoon ground cumin
- ¼ teaspoon ground cinnamon
- 1 (14-ounce) can light coconut milk
- 2 cups low-sodium vegetable broth
- Salt and pepper to taste
- Fresh cilantro for garnish (optional)

## Instructions:
1. In the slow cooker, combine red lentils, chopped onion, minced garlic, diced carrot, and diced sweet potato.
2. Add curry powder, ground cumin, and ground cinnamon. Stir to coat the vegetables and lentils with the spices.
3. Pour in the coconut milk and vegetable broth. Season with salt and pepper to taste.
4. Stir everything together until well combined.
5. Cover and cook on low for 4 hours, or until the lentils and vegetables are tender.
6. Before serving, taste and adjust seasoning as needed.
7. Serve hot, garnished with fresh cilantro if desired.

# Slow Cooker Balsamic Glazed Brussels Sprouts with Cranberries and Pecans

Preparation Time: 10 minutes
Cooking Time: 3 hours on low
Servings: 2

## Ingredients:

- 2 cups Brussels sprouts, trimmed and halved
- ¼ cup dried cranberries
- ¼ cup chopped pecans
- 2 tablespoons balsamic vinegar
- 1 tablespoon honey
- 1 tablespoon olive oil
- ½ teaspoon garlic powder
- Salt and pepper to taste

## Instructions:

1. In a small bowl, whisk together balsamic vinegar, honey, olive oil, garlic powder, salt, and pepper.
2. Add the halved Brussels sprouts to the slow cooker and pour the balsamic mixture over them. Toss to coat evenly.
3. Cover and cook on low for 3 hours or until the Brussels sprouts are tender.
4. Stir in dried cranberries and chopped pecans during the last 10 minutes of cooking.
5. Serve warm as a flavorful side or light lunch.

## Slow Cooker Lemon Herb Tilapia with Garlic Butter Green Beans

Preparation Time: 10 minutes

Cooking Time: 2 hours on low

Servings: 2

### Ingredients:

- 2 tilapia fillets (about 5-6 oz each)
- 1 cup fresh green beans, trimmed
- 2 tablespoons unsalted butter, melted
- 1 tablespoon fresh lemon juice
- 1 teaspoon lemon zest
- 1 teaspoon minced garlic
- ½ teaspoon dried oregano
- ½ teaspoon dried thyme
- Salt and pepper to taste
- Fresh parsley for garnish (optional)

### Instructions:

1. In a small bowl, mix melted butter, lemon juice, lemon zest, minced garlic, oregano, thyme, salt, and pepper.
2. Place the green beans in the bottom of the slow cooker. Lay the tilapia fillets on top.
3. Pour the garlic butter mixture over the tilapia and green beans.
4. Cover and cook on low for 2 hours or until the tilapia is flaky and the green beans are tender.
5. Serve immediately, garnished with fresh parsley if desired.

# CHAPTER THREE: DINNER RECIPES

## Slow Cooker Coq au Vin for Two

Servings: Two Portions
Preparation Time: 20 minutes
Cooking Time: 4–5 hours on low

### Ingredients
- 2 chicken thighs (bone-in, skin-on, about 1 pound total)
- 4 ounces cremini mushrooms, cut into quarters
- 1/2 medium onion, diced
- 1 medium carrot, sliced into rounds
- 2 small shallots, finely minced
- 2 garlic cloves, minced
- 1/2 cup dry red wine (e.g., Pinot Noir)
- 1/2 cup low-sodium chicken broth
- 1 tablespoon tomato paste
- 1 teaspoon dried thyme
- 1/2 teaspoon crushed bay leaf
- 1 tablespoon olive oil
- Salt and black pepper, to taste
- Optional: 1 tablespoon all-purpose flour mixed with 2 tablespoons cold water for thickening

### Instructions
1. Season the Chicken: Pat the chicken thighs dry and sprinkle both sides with salt and pepper. This helps the skin crisp up and enhances the flavor.
2. Sear the Chicken: Warm olive oil in a pan over medium-high heat. Place the chicken thighs skin-side down and cook until browned, about 3–4 minutes per side. Transfer to a plate.
3. Cook the Vegetables: In the same pan, add the mushrooms, onion, and carrots. Stir and cook until they soften slightly, about 5 minutes. Add the shallots and garlic, cooking for another minute. Transfer the mixture to your slow cooker.

4. Deglaze the Pan: Pour the red wine into the pan while it's still warm. Scrape the bottom to lift any browned bits—these will add depth to the sauce. Let it simmer for a minute.

5. Assemble in the Slow Cooker: Place the chicken thighs on top of the vegetables in the slow cooker. Add the wine mixture, chicken broth, tomato paste, thyme, and bay leaf. Stir gently to combine the flavors.

6. Cook: Cover the slow cooker and set it to low. Cook for 4–5 hours, or until the chicken is tender and the vegetables are soft. The chicken should reach an internal temperature of 165°F (74°C).

7. Thicken the Sauce (Optional): If you want a thicker sauce, mix flour with cold water to form a smooth paste. Add this mixture to the slow cooker in the last 15–20 minutes of cooking. Set the slow cooker to high, stirring occasionally until the sauce thickens

8. Serve: Spoon the chicken and vegetables onto plates and drizzle with the flavorful sauce. Serve immediately with bread, mashed potatoes, or your favorite side.

# Slow Cooker Moroccan Lamb with Apricots and Almonds

Servings: Two Portions
Prep Time: 20 minutes
Cook Time: 6–8 hours on low

## Ingredients

- 1/2 lb boneless lamb shoulder, trimmed and cut into 1-inch cubes
- 1/4 cup dried apricots, sliced in half
- 2 tablespoons slivered almonds
- 1/4 small yellow onion, finely chopped
- 1 clove garlic, minced
- 1/2 inch fresh ginger, grated
- 1/2 teaspoon ground cumin
- 1/4 teaspoon ground coriander
- 1/8 teaspoon ground turmeric
- 1/8 teaspoon ground cinnamon
- 1/8 cup low-sodium chicken broth
- 1/2 tablespoon honey
- 1 tablespoon olive oil
- Salt and freshly ground black pepper, to taste
- Fresh cilantro or parsley, chopped, for garnish

## Instructions

1. Prepare the Lamb: Heat olive oil in a skillet over medium-high heat. Lightly season the lamb cubes with salt and black pepper.
2. Brown the Meat: Place the lamb in the hot skillet in a single layer, avoiding overcrowding. Sear for 2–3 minutes on each side until the lamb is golden brown. Remove and set aside.
3. Sauté the Aromatics: In the same skillet, sauté the onion for about 3–4 minutes until softened. Add garlic and grated ginger, stirring frequently, and cook for 1 additional minute until fragrant.
4. Assemble in the Slow Cooker: Transfer the onion mixture to the slow cooker. Add the browned lamb, dried apricots, almonds, cumin, coriander,

turmeric, cinnamon, chicken broth, and honey. Stir to evenly combine all the flavors.

5. Cook the Dish: Cover and cook on low for 6–8 hours, or until the lamb is tender and can be easily pulled apart with a fork.

6. Finish the Sauce: Once the cooking is complete, shred the lamb gently in the slow cooker using two forks. Mix the shredded meat thoroughly with the sauce.

7. Garnish and Serve: Spoon the lamb and sauce into bowls. Garnish with fresh cilantro or parsley. Serve immediately, paired with couscous, rice, or crusty bread.

**Notes**
- Adjust seasoning (salt and pepper) after cooking if needed.
- This portion is specifically tailored for two servings without leftovers.

# Slow Cooker Beef Bourguignon

Portioning: Perfectly portioned for two satisfying servings.
Prep Time: 25 minutes
Cook Time: 6-8 hours on low

## Ingredients:
- 1 lb beef stew meat (preferably from chuck roast), cut into 1-inch cubes
- 4 oz pearl onions, peeled (alternatively, 1/2 medium yellow onion, cut into wedges)
- 4 oz cremini mushrooms, quartered
- 1 medium carrot, peeled and sliced
- 1/2 cup dry red wine (Burgundy or Pinot Noir recommended)
- 1 cup low-sodium beef broth
- 1 tablespoon tomato paste
- 1 teaspoon dried thyme
- 1/2 teaspoon dried bay leaf
- 1 tablespoon olive oil
- Salt and freshly ground black pepper, to taste
- 1 tablespoon all-purpose flour (optional, for thickening the sauce)

## Instructions:
1. Begin by patting the beef stew dry with paper towels to ensure proper browning. Season the meat generously with salt and freshly ground black pepper.
2. In a large skillet, heat the olive oil over medium-high heat. Brown the beef in batches, ensuring not to overcrowd the pan. Sear each side for approximately 2-3 minutes until a deep golden-brown crust forms. Once browned, transfer the beef to a plate and set aside.
3. In the same skillet, add the pearl onions (or onion wedges) and cook for about 5 minutes until lightly browned. Next, add the quartered mushrooms and sliced carrot, cooking for an additional 5 minutes until the vegetables soften.
4. Transfer both the browned beef and sautéed vegetables into the slow cooker.

5. Pour the dry red wine into the same skillet, and bring to a simmer over medium heat. Scrape up any browned bits from the bottom of the pan to incorporate the flavorful residues. Once the wine has simmered for a minute, pour the mixture into the slow cooker.

6. To the slow cooker, add the beef broth, tomato paste, dried thyme, and bay leaf. Stir gently to ensure even distribution of ingredients.

7. Cover the slow cooker and cook on low for 6-8 hours, or until the beef is tender and can be easily shredded with a fork.

8. For a thicker sauce, remove about 1/2 cup of the cooking liquid and whisk it with the flour in a small bowl to create a smooth slurry. Return the slurry to the slow cooker and stir well. Switch the slow cooker to high and cook for an additional 15-20 minutes until the sauce thickens to your desired consistency.

9. Before serving, remove the bay leaf and serve the Beef Bourguignon hot.

# Slow Cooker Duck Confit with Cherry Sauce (Tailored for Two)

Portioning: Two duck legs, perfectly sized.
Prep Time: 20 minutes (plus overnight curing)
Cook Time: 6-8 hours on low

## Ingredients:

- 2 duck legs (approximately 1 lb total)
- 1 tablespoon kosher salt
- 1/2 teaspoon freshly ground black pepper
- 1/4 teaspoon ground cloves
- 1/2 cup dry red wine (suggested: Pinot Noir or Merlot)
- 1/2 cup low-sodium chicken broth or duck stock
- 1/2 cup dried cherries, halved
- 1 tablespoon honey
- 1 small shallot, minced
- 1 sprig fresh thyme

## Instructions:

1. Cure the Duck (Overnight): Massage the duck legs with kosher salt, black pepper, and ground cloves. Seal them in a plastic bag or airtight container and refrigerate overnight. This step removes excess moisture, helping the skin become crispy, even in the slow cooker.
2. Prep for Cooking: The following day, rinse the duck legs under cold water to remove the salt. Pat them dry using paper towels.
3. Place in Slow Cooker: Position the duck legs in a single layer inside the slow cooker.
4. Make the Sauce: In a small mixing bowl, combine the dry red wine, chicken broth or duck stock, dried cherries, honey, minced shallot, and a sprig of fresh thyme.
5. Add Sauce to Duck: Pour the prepared cherry sauce evenly over the duck legs in the slow cooker.
6. Slow Cook: Cover and cook on low for 6-8 hours, or until the duck is tender and easily separates from the bone.

7. Optional Crisping for Presentation: If you'd like a crispy finish, carefully broil the duck legs, skin-side up, under a preheated broiler for about 2-3 minutes. Keep a close eye to avoid burning.
8. Serve: Serve hot and enjoy!

---

# Slow Cooker Pork Tenderloin with Fig and Port Sauce

Servings: Perfect for two people.
Prep Time: 15 minutes
Cook Time: 3-4 hours on low

## Ingredients:

- 1 (12-14 oz) pork tenderloin, trimmed of fat
- 1/3 cup dried figs, chopped
- 1/3 cup port wine
- 3 tablespoons low-sodium chicken broth
- 1 tablespoon balsamic vinegar
- 1 small shallot, finely chopped
- 1 sprig of fresh rosemary
- Salt and black pepper to taste

## Instructions:

1. Season the Pork: Sprinkle the pork tenderloin generously with salt and black pepper, ensuring all sides are evenly coated.

2. Prepare the Slow Cooker: Place the pork tenderloin into the slow cooker in a single layer.

3. Make the Sauce: In a small mixing bowl, combine the chopped figs, port wine, chicken broth, balsamic vinegar, chopped shallot, and rosemary. Stir until well mixed.

4. Add Sauce to the Cooker: Pour the fig and port mixture over the pork tenderloin, ensuring the meat is coated evenly.

5. Cook the Pork: Cover the slow cooker and set it to low. Cook for 3-4 hours, or until the pork reaches an internal temperature of 145°F (63°C). Use a meat thermometer to ensure it's cooked perfectly.

6. Rest the Pork: Take the pork out of the slow cooker and transfer it to a cutting board. Allow it to rest for 10 minutes to retain its juices before slicing.

7. Reduce the Sauce (Optional): If you'd like a thicker sauce, remove the lid from the slow cooker and set it high. Let the sauce simmer for 15-20 minutes or until slightly reduced. Stir occasionally to prevent burning.

8. Serve: Slice the pork tenderloin into medallions and plate it. Drizzle the fig and port sauce over the top before serving.

---

# Slow Cooker Halibut with Mango Salsa (For Two)

Servings: Perfectly portioned for two
Prep Time: 15 minutes
Cook Time: 1–1.5 hours on low

## Ingredients:
### For the Halibut:
- 2 halibut fillets, 6 ounces each (skin-on helps retain moisture, but skinless works too)
- Olive oil or non-stick cooking spray (for greasing)
- Salt and black pepper, to taste

### For the Mango Salsa:
- 1 medium mango, peeled and chopped into small pieces
- 2 tablespoons red onion, finely diced
- 1/4 small jalapeño, seeds removed and finely chopped (optional for some spice)
- 2 tablespoons fresh cilantro, chopped
- Juice from half a lime (adjust to taste)
- Small pinch of salt

## Instructions

1. Prepare the Salsa: Combine the mango, red onion, jalapeño (if using), cilantro, lime juice, and salt in a bowl. Mix gently until well combined. Set the salsa aside to let the flavors blend while you cook the fish.

2. Prepare the Slow Cooker: Lightly coat the bottom of the slow cooker with olive oil or cooking spray to prevent the fish from sticking.

3. Add the Halibut: Arrange the halibut fillets in a single layer inside the slow cooker. Sprinkle them lightly with salt and black pepper for seasoning.

4. Cook the Halibut: Cover and cook the fish on low for 1–1.5 hours. Start checking after 1 hour to avoid overcooking. The fish is ready when it easily flakes apart with a fork but remains juicy.

5. Serve: Gently remove the halibut fillets from the slow cooker and place them onto plates. Spoon the mango salsa over the fillets and serve right away.

# Slow Cooker Chicken with Preserved Lemons and Olives

Servings: Two Portions
Prep Time: 15 minutes
Cook Time: 4–6 hours on low

## Ingredients:

- 2 medium chicken thighs, boneless and skinless (about 1 lb total)
- 2 tablespoons preserved lemon peel, rinsed and finely chopped (discard the flesh)
- 1/4 cup green olives, halved (Kalamata olives can also be used)
- 1/4 small yellow onion, finely diced
- 1 clove garlic, minced
- 1/4 cup low-sodium chicken broth
- 1/2 teaspoon ground cumin
- 1/4 teaspoon ground coriander
- 1/8 teaspoon ground turmeric
- A pinch of red pepper flakes (optional, for heat)
- Chopped fresh parsley or cilantro, for garnish

## Instructions:

1. Prepare the Chicken: Place the chicken thighs in a single layer at the bottom of the slow cooker.
2. Make the Sauce: In a small bowl, mix the preserved lemon peel, halved olives, diced onion, minced garlic, chicken broth, cumin, coriander, turmeric, and red pepper flakes (if using).
3. Add the Sauce: Pour the prepared mixture evenly over the chicken thighs in the slow cooker.
4. Cook: Cover the slow cooker and set it to low. Cook for 4–6 hours, or until the chicken is fully cooked and tender enough to shred with a fork.
5. Shred the Chicken: Remove the chicken from the slow cooker and use two forks to shred it into smaller pieces.
6. Combine: Return the shredded chicken to the slow cooker and stir it into the sauce to ensure the flavors are well combined.
7. Garnish and Serve: Sprinkle with fresh parsley or cilantro before serving.

# Slow Cooker Vegetarian Tagine with Dates and Almonds

Portioning: Two servings
Prep Time: 20 minutes
Cook Time: 4–6 hours on low

## Ingredients:
- 1 small sweet potato (about 1/2 pound), peeled and diced into 1/2-inch cubes
- 1/2 (15-ounce) can chickpeas, rinsed and drained (about 3/4 cup)
- 1/2 (14.5-ounce) can diced tomatoes, undrained (about 3/4 cup)
- 1/4 cup pitted dates, chopped
- 2 tablespoons slivered almonds
- 1/2 medium yellow onion, chopped
- 1 clove garlic, minced
- 1/2 inch fresh ginger, grated
- 1/2 teaspoon ground cumin
- 1/4 teaspoon ground coriander
- 1/8 teaspoon ground cinnamon
- 1/8 teaspoon ground turmeric
- 2 tablespoons low-sodium vegetable broth
- 1 teaspoon olive oil
- Salt and freshly ground black pepper, to taste
- Chopped fresh cilantro or parsley, for garnish (optional)

## Instructions:
1. Sauté Aromatics: Heat the olive oil in a skillet over medium heat. Add the chopped onion and cook for about 3–4 minutes, until softened. Stir in the minced garlic and grated ginger and cook for another minute until fragrant.
2. Assemble Ingredients: Transfer the sautéed mixture to the slow cooker. Add the diced sweet potato, chickpeas, diced tomatoes (with their juices), chopped dates, slivered almonds, cumin, coriander, cinnamon, turmeric, vegetable broth, salt, and black pepper.
3. Mix and Cook: Stir everything well to combine. Cover the slow cooker and cook on low for 4–6 hours, or until the sweet potato is tender and easily pierced with a fork.

4. Taste and Adjust: Once cooked, taste the tagine and adjust seasoning with more salt and pepper if needed. You can also add a small squeeze of lemon juice for extra brightness.

5. Serve: Spoon the tagine into bowls and garnish with fresh cilantro or parsley if desired. Serve on its own or pair with couscous or quinoa for a complete meal.

# CHAPTER FOUR: SOUPS AND STEWS RECIPES

## SOUPS RECIPES

### Slow Cooker Sweet Potato, Apple, and Ginger Soup with Toasted Pumpkin Seeds

Servings: Two bowls
Prep Time: 15 minutes
Cook Time: 4–6 hours on low

**Ingredients:**
- 1 small sweet potato, peeled and cubed
- 1 small apple (like Honeycrisp or Gala), peeled, cored, and diced
- ½ small yellow onion, chopped
- 1 clove garlic, minced
- ½ inch fresh ginger, grated
- 2 cups vegetable broth
- 2 tablespoons full-fat coconut milk
- Salt and black pepper, to taste
- 1 tablespoon pumpkin seeds (pepitas), toasted

**Instructions:**
1. Combine Ingredients: Add the cubed sweet potato, chopped apple, onion, garlic, ginger, and vegetable broth to the slow cooker. Sprinkle in some salt and black pepper to taste.
2. Cook Until Tender: Cover and cook on low for 4–6 hours, or until the sweet potato and apple are soft.
3. Blend Until Smooth: Use an immersion blender to puree the soup until silky and smooth.
4. Stir in Coconut Milk: Add the coconut milk and stir well. Let it heat through for a few minutes without boiling.
5. Serve and Garnish: Pour the soup into two bowls and sprinkle each with toasted pumpkin seeds for added crunch.

## Slow Cooker Carrot, Orange, and Turmeric Soup with Candied Ginger

Serving Size: Two Portions
Preparation Time:
Prep: 15 minutes
Cook: 4 to 6 hours on low

### Ingredients:

- 1 pound carrots, peeled and chopped
- Zest and juice of 1 large orange
- 1 small yellow onion, finely chopped
- 2 cloves garlic, minced
- 1-inch piece of fresh ginger, grated
- ½ teaspoon ground turmeric
- 4 cups vegetable broth
- Salt and freshly ground black pepper, to taste
- 2 tablespoons candied ginger, finely chopped (for garnish)

### Instructions:

1. Prepare the base: In the slow cooker, combine the carrots, orange zest and juice, onion, garlic, ginger, turmeric, and vegetable broth. Season with salt and black pepper to taste.
2. Slow cook: Cover and cook on low heat for 4 to 6 hours, or until the carrots are exceptionally tender.
3. Blend to perfection: Using an immersion blender, puree the soup until silky smooth. If a creamier texture is desired, adjust the consistency with additional broth.
4. Serve and garnish: Ladle the soup into bowls and top with finely chopped candied ginger for a hint of sweetness and spice. Serve immediately.

# Slow Cooker Tomato and Roasted Red Pepper Bisque with Basil Oil

Serving Size: Yields two bowls.
Prep: 15 minutes
Cook: 4 to 6 hours on low

## Ingredients:
### For the Bisque:
- 1 (14.5-ounce) can crushed tomatoes (adjusted from 28 oz for two servings)
- 1 red bell pepper, roasted (roast ahead for enhanced depth) and chopped
- ½ small yellow onion, finely chopped
- 1 clove garlic, minced
- ½ teaspoon dried oregano
- ¼ cup heavy cream or full-fat coconut milk (for a vegan alternative)
- Salt and freshly ground black pepper, to taste

### For the Basil Oil:
- 2 tablespoons fresh basil leaves, finely chopped
- 2 tablespoons extra virgin olive oil

## Instructions:
1. Prepare the base: In the slow cooker, combine crushed tomatoes, roasted red pepper, onion, garlic, and oregano. Season with salt and black pepper.
2. Slow cook: Cover and cook on low heat for 4 to 6 hours, allowing the flavors to meld beautifully.
3. Make the basil oil: While the soup is cooking, blend basil leaves and olive oil in a food processor until smooth. Set aside.
4. Blend the bisque: Once the vegetables are tender, use an immersion blender to puree the soup until silky smooth. Stir in the heavy cream or coconut milk for added richness
5. Serve and garnish: Ladle the bisque into two bowls and drizzle each with basil oil before serving.

# Slow Cooker Creamy Corn and Jalapeño Chowder with Lime Crema

Portioning: Serves two.
Prep Time: 15 minutes
Cook Time: 3-4 hours on low

## Ingredients:
- **For the Chowder:**
  - 3 cups frozen corn kernels
  - 1 small yellow onion, chopped
  - 2 cloves garlic, minced
  - 1 jalapeño, deseeded and finely chopped (adjust to desired spice level)
  - 3 cups vegetable broth
  - 1/3 cup heavy cream or full-fat coconut milk (for vegan option)
  - Salt and pepper to taste

- **For the Lime Crema:**
  - 3 tablespoons sour cream or Greek yogurt (substitute with vegan yogurt if needed)
  - 1 tablespoon lime juice
  - 1 tablespoon fresh cilantro, chopped

## Instructions:
1. In the slow cooker, combine the corn, onion, garlic, jalapeño, and vegetable broth. Season with salt and pepper.
2. Cover and cook on low for 3-4 hours until the vegetables are soft.
3. Use an immersion blender to blend the soup to a smooth consistency. Stir in the heavy cream or coconut milk.
4. While the soup is cooking, mix the sour cream (or yogurt), lime juice, and cilantro in a small bowl to make the lime crema.
5. Serve the soup hot with a generous dollop of lime crema on top.

# Slow Cooker Curried Pumpkin and Pear Soup with Toasted Almonds

Portioning: Two servings.
Prep Time: 15 minutes
Cook Time: 4-6 hours on low

## Ingredients:
- **For the Soup:**
  - 1 (10-ounce) can pumpkin puree
  - 1 medium pear (such as Bartlett), peeled, cored, and chopped
  - 1 small yellow onion, chopped
  - 1 clove garlic, minced
  - 1 inch fresh ginger, grated
  - 1/2 tablespoon curry powder
  - 1/4 teaspoon ground cumin
  - 1/8 teaspoon ground coriander
  - 3 cups vegetable broth
  - 3 tablespoons coconut milk (full-fat)
  - Salt and pepper to taste

- **For Garnish:**
  - 1 tablespoon slivered almonds, toasted

## Instructions:
1. In the slow cooker, combine pumpkin puree, chopped pear, onion, garlic, ginger, curry powder, cumin, coriander, and vegetable broth. Season with salt and pepper.
2. Cover and cook on low for 4-6 hours, until the pear is very tender.
3. Use an immersion blender to blend the soup until smooth. Stir in the coconut milk for creaminess.
4. Serve hot, garnished with toasted slivered almonds.

# STEW RECIPES

## Slow Cooker Beef and Fig Stew with Balsamic Glaze

Serving Size: Makes exactly two servings.
Preparation Time: 25 minutes
Cook Time: 6-8 hours on low

**Ingredients:**
- 3/4 lb beef stew chunks (chuck roast is ideal), cut into small 1-inch pieces
- 1/3 cup dried figs, cut into quarters
- 1 small red onion, chopped
- 1 medium carrot, peeled and sliced
- 1 celery stalk, chopped
- 1 garlic clove, finely chopped
- 3/4 cup low-sodium beef broth
- 3 tablespoons balsamic vinegar
- 2 teaspoons tomato paste
- 3/4 teaspoon dried thyme
- 1/3 teaspoon dried rosemary
- 2 teaspoons olive oil
- 1/3 teaspoon brown sugar (for added sweetness)
- Salt and freshly cracked black pepper, to taste

**Instructions:**
1. Begin by patting the beef dry with paper towels, ensuring it's free of excess moisture. Season with salt and freshly cracked black pepper on all sides.
2. Heat olive oil in a large skillet over medium-high heat. Brown the beef in small batches, allowing each piece to get a good sear, which adds flavor. Once browned, transfer the beef to a plate and set it aside.
3. In the same skillet, add the chopped onion, carrot, and celery. Sauté for about 5-6 minutes, or until the vegetables soften. Add in the minced garlic and cook for another minute until fragrant.

4. Transfer the sautéed vegetables to the slow cooker. Then, add the browned beef, chopped figs, beef broth, balsamic vinegar, tomato paste, thyme, rosemary, and brown sugar. Stir everything together to combine.
5. Place the lid on the slow cooker and cook on low for 6-8 hours, or until the beef is tender and can be easily shredded with a fork.
6. Once the stew is ready, taste it and adjust the seasoning with salt and pepper as needed.
7. Serve the stew hot, making sure each serving includes the rich balsamic glaze and figs.

---

## Slow Cooker Chicken Tagine with Apricots and Couscous

Serving Size: Two Portions
Preparation Time: 20 minutes
Cooking Time: 4-6 hours on low

**Ingredients:**
- 1 lb boneless, skinless chicken thighs (around 2-3 pieces)
- 1/2 cup dried apricots, cut in half
- 1 small yellow onion, diced
- 1 red bell pepper, diced
- 1 (14.5-ounce) can of diced tomatoes, undrained
- 1/2 cup low-sodium chicken broth
- 1 tablespoon honey
- 1 teaspoon ground cumin
- 1/2 teaspoon ground coriander
- 1/4 teaspoon ground cinnamon
- A pinch of saffron threads (optional)
- Salt and pepper, to taste
- 1/3 cup couscous

**Instructions:**
1. Place the chicken thighs in the base of the slow cooker.
2. In a bowl, mix the halved apricots, diced onion, red bell pepper, undrained tomatoes, chicken broth, honey, cumin, coriander, cinnamon, saffron (if using), salt, and pepper.
3. Pour the prepared mixture over the chicken in the slow cooker, ensuring everything is evenly covered.
4. Cover the slow cooker and cook on low for 4-6 hours, or until the chicken is tender and fully cooked. Once the chicken is ready, shred it with two forks and stir it into the sauce.
5. Meanwhile, prepare the couscous according to the instructions on the package (typically, you'll bring water to a boil, pour it over the couscous, cover it, and let it sit for about 5 minutes). Fluff the couscous with a fork after it's done.

6. Serve the chicken and apricot mixture on top of the couscous and enjoy!

---

# Slow Cooker Lentil and Sweet Potato Stew with Spinach

Serves: Two perfect portions
Preparation Time: 15 minutes
Cooking Time: 4-6 hours on low

## Ingredients:
- 2/3 cup red lentils, rinsed and drained
- 1 medium sweet potato, peeled and cut into small cubes
- 2/3 cup full-fat coconut milk (for a creamy texture)
- 1.5-2 cups vegetable broth (depending on how thick you like it)
- 1 small yellow onion, finely chopped
- 2 garlic cloves, minced
- 1-inch piece of fresh ginger, grated
- 1 tablespoon curry powder
- 1/2 teaspoon ground cumin
- 1/4 teaspoon turmeric powder
- 5 ounces fresh spinach, roughly chopped
- Salt and black pepper, to taste

## Instructions:
1. Prepare the Base: Add the lentils, diced sweet potato, coconut milk, vegetable broth, chopped onion, minced garlic, grated ginger, curry powder, cumin, and turmeric to the slow cooker. Season with salt and pepper, then stir everything to combine evenly.
2. Cook: Cover the slow cooker and set it to low. Let it cook for 4-6 hours, or until the lentils are soft and the sweet potato pieces are tender.
3. Add Spinach: About 30 minutes before the stew is ready, stir in the spinach. Allow it to wilt gently into the stew during the remaining cooking time.
4. Serve: Ladle the hot stew into bowls and serve immediately.

# Slow Cooker Lentil and Sweet Potato Curry with Spinach

Serves: Two hearty portions
Prep Time: 15 minutes
Cook Time: 4-6 hours on low

## Ingredients:

- 2/3 cup red lentils, rinsed and drained
- 1 small sweet potato, peeled and diced into small cubes
- 1 cup full-fat coconut milk
- 2 cups vegetable broth (add more for desired consistency)
- 1 small yellow onion, finely chopped
- 2 garlic cloves, minced
- 1 teaspoon freshly grated ginger
- 2 teaspoons curry powder
- 1/4 teaspoon ground cumin
- 1/4 teaspoon turmeric powder
- 3 oz fresh spinach, chopped
- Salt and black pepper, to taste

## Instructions:

1. Prepare Ingredients: Add the red lentils, diced sweet potato, coconut milk, vegetable broth, onion, garlic, ginger, curry powder, cumin, turmeric, salt, and pepper to the slow cooker. Stir to combine.
2. Cook the Base: Cover the slow cooker and set it to low heat. Let it cook for 4-6 hours, or until the sweet potato pieces are soft and the lentils are fully tender.
3. Add Spinach: About 30 minutes before the cooking time ends, stir in the chopped spinach. Allow it to wilt into the curry.
4. Final Touches: Taste the curry and adjust the seasoning with additional salt or pepper, if necessary. Serve warm, either on its own or with a side of flatbread or rice.

## Slow Cooker Honey-Glazed Pork with Apples and Cabbage

Serves: Two portions
Prep Time: 15 minutes
Cook Time: 4-6 hours on low

### Ingredients:
- 2/3 lb pork tenderloin or boneless pork loin, trimmed
- 1 medium apple, cored and thinly sliced
- 1/4 small head of green cabbage, finely shredded
- 1/2 small yellow onion, finely chopped
- 2 tablespoons honey
- 1 tablespoon apple cider vinegar
- 1 teaspoon Dijon mustard
- 1/4 teaspoon caraway seeds
- 1 teaspoon apple juice or cider
- Salt and black pepper, to taste

### Instructions:
1. Layer the Base: Place the shredded cabbage and chopped onion at the bottom of the slow cooker to create a flavorful base.
2. Add Pork and Apples: Place the pork tenderloin on top of the cabbage mixture. Arrange the apple slices around the pork.
3. Prepare the Glaze: In a small bowl, whisk together honey, apple cider vinegar, Dijon mustard, apple juice, caraway seeds, salt, and pepper. Pour this mixture evenly over the pork and vegetables.
4. Cook: Cover and cook on low for 4-6 hours, or until the pork reaches an internal temperature of 145°F (63°C).
5. Rest and Serve: Once cooked, remove the pork from the slow cooker and let it rest for 10 minutes before slicing. Serve warm with the cabbage and apples on the side.

# CHAPTER FIVE: POULTRY RECIPES

## Slow Cooker Chicken with Fig and Balsamic Glaze

Serves: Two portions
Prep Time: 15 minutes
Cook Time: 4-6 hours on low

### Ingredients:
- 2 medium boneless, skinless chicken thighs (about 2/3 lb)
- 1/3 cup dried figs, quartered
- 3 tablespoons balsamic vinegar
- 1/3 cup low-sodium chicken broth
- 2 teaspoons honey
- 1 small shallot, minced
- 1 small sprig of fresh thyme
- 1/4 teaspoon orange zest
- Salt and freshly ground black pepper to taste

### Instructions:
1. Season the Chicken: Sprinkle the chicken thighs with salt and black pepper on both sides.
2. Prepare the Slow Cooker: Place the chicken thighs at the bottom of the slow cooker.
3. Mix the Sauce: In a small bowl, combine the quartered dried figs, balsamic vinegar, chicken broth, honey, minced shallot, thyme sprig, and orange zest. Stir well to mix.
4. Add Sauce to the Cooker: Pour the sauce mixture evenly over the chicken thighs.
5. Cook: Cover the slow cooker and cook on low for 4-6 hours, or until the chicken is tender and shreds easily with a fork.

# Slow Cooker Honey Mustard Chicken with Apples and Onions

Servings: Makes two portions
Preparation Time: 15 minutes
Cooking Time: 4-6 hours on low

## Ingredients:

- 2 medium chicken thighs or breasts (about 2/3 lb total, use thighs for juicier results)
- 1 medium apple, cored and thinly sliced (choose a sweet variety like Gala or Honeycrisp)
- 1 small yellow onion, sliced
- 3 tablespoons of honey
- 1 1/2 tablespoons Dijon mustard
- 1 teaspoon apple cider vinegar
- 1/4 teaspoon dried thyme
- A pinch of ground cinnamon (for warmth and sweetness)
- Salt and pepper to taste

## Instructions:

1. Prepare the Base: Spread the sliced onion across the bottom of your slow cooker, then arrange the apple slices over the onion.
2. Season and Arrange the Chicken: Lay the chicken thighs or breasts on top of the onion and apples.
3. Mix the Sauce: In a small mixing bowl, whisk together honey, Dijon mustard, apple cider vinegar, thyme, cinnamon, and a pinch of salt and pepper until smooth and well blended.
4. Pour and Cook: Pour the sauce evenly over the chicken, ensuring everything is coated. Cover the slow cooker and set it to cook on low for 4-6 hours, or until the chicken is tender and cooked through.

# Slow Cooker Chicken and Sweet Potato Curry

Portion Size: Two Portions
Prep Time: 15 minutes
Cook Time: 4-6 hours on low

## Ingredients:
- 1 lb boneless, skinless chicken thighs
- 1 medium sweet potato, peeled and diced into bite-sized pieces
- 1 (14-ounce) can of full-fat coconut milk for a creamy texture
- 1 small yellow onion, finely chopped
- 1 inch of fresh ginger, grated
- 1 tablespoon curry powder
- 1/2 teaspoon ground cumin
- 1/4 teaspoon turmeric
- 1/2 teaspoon honey (to enhance the natural sweetness)
- Salt and black pepper to taste

## Instructions:
1. Layer the Ingredients: Place the chicken thighs in the bottom of your slow cooker. Add the diced sweet potato, chopped onion, and grated ginger.
2. Mix the Seasoning: In a small bowl, combine the curry powder, cumin, turmeric, honey, salt, and pepper. Pour the coconut milk into the bowl and whisk everything together until smooth.
3. Pour Over Chicken: Gently pour the seasoned coconut milk mixture over the chicken and vegetables in the slow cooker, ensuring everything is evenly coated.
4. Cook Slowly: Cover and cook on low for 4-6 hours. The chicken should be tender and easy to shred, and the sweet potatoes should be soft and flavorful.
5. Serve and Enjoy: Taste and adjust seasoning with additional salt or pepper. Serve warm on its own or over a bed of steamed rice or quinoa for a complete meal.

# Slow Cooker Turkey with Cranberry-Orange Sauce and Wild Rice

Serving Size: Makes two servings.
Preparation Time: 20 minutes
Cooking Time: 4-6 hours on low

## Ingredients:

- 1 lb boneless, skinless turkey thighs or tenderloin (cut into 1-inch pieces)
- 1 cup fresh or frozen cranberries
- 1 large orange, zest and juice (approximately 1/2 cup juice)
- 1/2 cup low-sodium chicken or turkey broth
- 2 tablespoons honey or maple syrup
- 1 small shallot, finely chopped
- 1/2 teaspoon ground ginger
- 1/4 teaspoon ground cloves
- 1/4 teaspoon orange extract (optional, for added citrus aroma)
- Salt and pepper, to taste
- 1/2 cup cooked wild rice (for serving)

## Instructions:

1. Prepare the turkey: Season the turkey pieces with salt and pepper.
2. Make the sauce: In the slow cooker, combine cranberries, orange zest, orange juice, broth, honey or maple syrup, shallot, ginger, cloves, and orange extract (if using). Stir everything together to mix.
3. Add turkey: Place the seasoned turkey into the slow cooker, covering it with the sauce mixture.
4. Cook: Cover and cook on low for 4-6 hours, or until the turkey is tender and shreds easily with a fork.
5. Prepare the rice: While the turkey is cooking, prepare the wild rice according to the package instructions.
6. Serve: Once the turkey is ready, serve it over the cooked wild rice and enjoy!

# Slow Cooker Turkey and Sweet Potato Chili with Chipotle

Servings: Two hearty portions
Prep Time: 20 minutes
Cook Time: 4-6 hours on low

## Ingredients:

- 1/2 pound ground turkey (lean, yet flavorful)
- 1/2 medium sweet potato, peeled and diced into bite-sized cubes
- 1/2 can (15-ounce) diced tomatoes, with their juices (use fire-roasted for more depth)
- 1/2 can (15-ounce) black beans, rinsed and drained
- 1/2 small yellow onion, finely chopped
- 1 chipotle pepper in adobo, finely minced (use more or less depending on your heat preference)
- 1 tablespoon chili powder (adds a bold, spicy base)
- 1/2 teaspoon ground cumin (earthy and warm)
- 1/4 teaspoon smoked paprika (a subtle, smoky note)
- 1/8 teaspoon ground cinnamon (a hint of sweetness and warmth)
- 1 teaspoon unsweetened cocoa powder (enhances the overall flavor)
- 1/2 tablespoon maple syrup or brown sugar (balances the spices with a touch of sweetness)
- Salt and freshly ground black pepper, to taste

## Instructions:

1. Cook the turkey: In a skillet over medium heat, brown the ground turkey, breaking it up into small pieces as it cooks. Once fully browned, drain any excess fat if needed.

2. Load the slow cooker: Add the cooked turkey to your slow cooker along with the sweet potato, diced tomatoes, black beans, chopped onion, and minced chipotle pepper.

3. Season and mix: Sprinkle in the chili powder, cumin, smoked paprika, cinnamon, and cocoa powder. Drizzle the maple syrup on top, then season with salt and pepper. Stir everything together to ensure the ingredients are evenly combined.

4. Set and cook: Cover the slow cooker and cook on low heat for 4-6 hours, or until the sweet potatoes are tender and the flavors have blended beautifully. Stir occasionally if you can.

5. Taste and adjust: Before serving, taste the chili and adjust the seasoning if needed. Add more salt, pepper, or a little extra sweetness if desired.

6. Serve hot: Divide the chili into two bowls and enjoy. For added flair, top with fresh cilantro, diced avocado, a dollop of sour cream, or a sprinkle of shredded cheese.

---

# Slow Cooker Turkey Meatballs with Apple Cider Glaze

Portioning: Serves two with plenty of meatballs and sauce.
Prep Time: 25 minutes
Cook Time: 3-4 hours on low

## Ingredients:
- **For the Meatballs:**
    - 1 lb ground turkey
    - 1/4 cup panko breadcrumbs (for a light texture)
    - 1 egg, beaten
    - 1/4 small onion, finely chopped
    - 1 garlic clove, minced
    - 1 tablespoon fresh parsley, chopped
    - 1/4 teaspoon ground allspice (adds warmth)
    - Salt and pepper to taste

- **For the Glaze:**
    - 1 cup apple cider
    - 2 tablespoons honey
    - 1 tablespoon Dijon mustard
    - 1 tablespoon apple cider vinegar
    - 1 tablespoon apple butter

## Instructions:
1. Prepare the meatballs: In a large bowl, mix the turkey, panko breadcrumbs, beaten egg, onion, garlic, parsley, allspice, salt, and pepper. Shape the mixture into small meatballs.
2. Make the glaze: In the slow cooker, whisk together the apple cider, honey, Dijon mustard, apple cider vinegar, and apple butter until combined.
3. Cook the meatballs: Gently add the formed meatballs into the glaze in the slow cooker.
4. Simmer: Cover and cook on low for 3-4 hours, or until the meatballs are fully cooked through and tender.

# Slow Cooker Turkey and Quinoa Stuffed Bell Peppers

Servings: Two portions (two stuffed peppers).
Prep Time: 25 minutes
Cook Time: 4-6 hours on low

## Ingredients:
- 2 large bell peppers (any color), halved and seeds removed
- 1/2 lb ground turkey
- 1/4 cup cooked quinoa
- 1 small onion, finely chopped
- 1 clove garlic, minced
- 3/4 cup tomato sauce (divided)
- 1/2 teaspoon dried oregano
- 1/4 teaspoon ground cumin
- 1/2 tablespoon brown sugar
- Salt and black pepper to taste
- 2 tablespoons shredded cheddar cheese (optional)

## Instructions:
1. Heat a skillet over medium heat. Cook the ground turkey until browned, breaking it into small pieces. Drain any excess fat and set aside.

2. In a bowl, mix the cooked turkey, quinoa, onion, garlic, 1/2 cup of tomato sauce, oregano, cumin, brown sugar, salt, and pepper. Stir until evenly combined.

3. Stuff the mixture into the halved bell peppers, packing it tightly but without overfilling.

4. Place the stuffed peppers in the slow cooker, ensuring they fit snugly. Pour the remaining 1/4 cup of tomato sauce over the peppers.

5. Cover and cook on low for 4-6 hours, or until the peppers are tender and easily pierced with a fork.

6. If desired, sprinkle the tops with cheddar cheese during the last 30 minutes of cooking and allow it to melt.

7. Serve warm and enjoy!

# Slow Cooker Turkey Breast with Peach and Bourbon Glaze

Servings: Two generous portions
Prep Time: 15 minutes
Cook Time: 4-6 hours on low

## Ingredients:

- 1 lb boneless, skinless turkey breast
- 7-8 ounces canned peaches in juice, drained (reserve 1/4 cup juice)
- 1/4 cup bourbon
- 1 tablespoon honey
- 1 teaspoon Dijon mustard
- 1 small shallot, finely chopped
- 1 small sprig of fresh rosemary
- 1/8 teaspoon ground cinnamon
- Salt and freshly ground black pepper to taste

## Instructions:

1. Prepare the turkey: Season the breast generously with salt and pepper on all sides.

2. Mix the glaze: In the slow cooker, whisk together the reserved peach juice, bourbon, honey, Dijon mustard, chopped shallot, rosemary, and cinnamon until combined.

3. Assemble the dish: Place the seasoned turkey breast into the slow cooker. Arrange the sliced peaches around the turkey to evenly distribute the flavor.

4. Cook the turkey: Cover the slow cooker with the lid and cook on low for 4-6 hours, or until the turkey reaches an internal temperature of 165°F.

5. Let it rest: Once the turkey is done, carefully remove it from the slow cooker and rest for 5-10 minutes before slicing.

6. Serve and enjoy: Slice the turkey breast and serve it with the peach slices. Drizzle the glaze from the slow cooker over the turkey for extra flavor.

**Notes:**
This dish is perfectly portioned for two, ensuring no leftovers. The bourbon and peaches create a sweet, tangy glaze that pairs beautifully with the tender turkey, making it both delicious and satisfying.

---

# CHAPTER SIX: BEEF AND PORK RECIPES

## Slow Cooker Korean Beef Short Ribs

Portioning: Two hearty servings.
Prep Time: 20 minutes
Cook Time: 6-8 hours on low

**Ingredients:**

- 1 lb bone-in beef short ribs, cut into 2-inch pieces
- 1/4 cup low-sodium soy sauce or tamari
- 2 tablespoons light brown sugar
- 1 tablespoon rice vinegar
- 1 small Asian pear or a firm apple, peeled, cored, and grated
- 2 cloves garlic, minced
- 1-inch piece of fresh ginger, grated
- 1/2 teaspoon sesame oil
- 1/4 teaspoon red pepper flakes (adjust based on spice preference)
- Salt and freshly ground black pepper, to taste

**Instructions:**

1. Season the beef short ribs with a generous amount of salt and freshly ground black pepper.

2. In your slow cooker, mix the soy sauce (or tamari), brown sugar, rice vinegar, grated pear or apple, minced garlic, grated ginger, sesame oil, and red pepper flakes.

3. Add the short ribs to the slow cooker, ensuring the meat is fully coated with the sauce mixture.

4. Cover and cook on low for 6-8 hours, until the meat becomes tender and falls off the bone.

# Slow Cooker Beef and Sweet Potato Curry with Coconut Milk

Serving Size: Makes 2 satisfying servings.
Prep Time: 15 minutes
Cook Time: 4-6 hours on low

**Ingredients:**

- 3/4 lb beef stew meat, cut into 1-inch cubes
- 1 medium sweet potato, peeled and diced into 1/2-inch pieces
- 1 (14-ounce) can full-fat coconut milk (for a rich, creamy texture)
- 3 cups low-sodium beef or vegetable broth
- 1 small yellow onion, chopped
- 1 inch fresh ginger, grated
- 1 tablespoon curry powder
- 1/2 teaspoon ground cumin
- 1/4 teaspoon ground turmeric
- 1/2 teaspoon honey
- Juice of half a lime (added at the end)
- Salt and freshly ground black pepper to taste

**Instructions:**

1. Season the beef with salt and freshly ground black pepper to your liking.
2. In the slow cooker, add the sweet potato, coconut milk, broth, onion, ginger, curry powder, cumin, turmeric, and honey. Stir to combine.
3. Add the seasoned beef to the slow cooker and mix it in with the other ingredients.
4. Cover the slow cooker and cook on low for 4-6 hours, or until the beef is tender and the sweet potato is fully cooked.
5. Just before serving, stir in the lime juice to brighten the flavor.

# Slow Cooker Beef and Apple Stew with Cider and Thyme

Portioning: Serves two
Prep Time: 20 minutes
Cook Time: 4-6 hours on low

## Ingredients:

- 3/4 lb beef stew meat, cut into 1-inch chunks
- 2 medium apples (such as Honeycrisp or Gala), cored and diced
- 1 small yellow onion, chopped
- 1 cup apple cider
- 1/2 cup low-sodium beef broth
- 1 tablespoon honey
- 1 tablespoon Dijon mustard
- 1 teaspoon dried thyme
- 1/4 teaspoon ground allspice
- Salt and freshly ground black pepper, to taste

## Instructions:

1. Season the beef with salt and black pepper to taste.
2. In the slow cooker, add the chopped apples, onion, apple cider, beef broth, honey, Dijon mustard, dried thyme, and ground allspice.
3. Stir everything together and add the seasoned beef to the slow cooker.
4. Cover the cooker and let it cook on low for 4-6 hours, or until the beef is tender and the flavors have combined beautifully.

## Slow Cooker Beef and Apricot Tagine with Almonds

Serves: Two Portions
Prep Time: 20 minutes
Cook Time: 6-8 hours on low

### Ingredients:

- 3/4 lb beef stew meat (preferably chuck or round), cut into 1-inch cubes
- 1/3 cup dried apricots, halved
- 1 small yellow onion, chopped
- 2 cloves garlic, minced
- 1-inch piece of fresh ginger, grated
- 1/2 cup low-sodium beef broth
- 1 tablespoon honey
- 1 teaspoon ground cumin
- 1/2 teaspoon ground coriander
- 1/4 teaspoon ground cinnamon
- 1/4 cup slivered almonds, toasted (for garnish)
- 1 tablespoon olive oil
- Salt and freshly ground black pepper, to taste
- 1/4 teaspoon orange zest (for added fruity flavor)

### Instructions:

1. Begin by patting the beef dry using paper towels, then season it generously with salt and freshly ground black pepper.

2. Heat olive oil in a large skillet over medium-high heat. Brown the beef in batches to ensure it gets a good sear. Be careful not to overcrowd the pan. Once browned, remove the beef from the skillet and set it aside.

3. In the same skillet, add the chopped onion and sauté for about 5 minutes until softened. Then, stir in the minced garlic and grated ginger, cooking for an additional minute until fragrant.

4. Transfer the sautéed vegetables into the slow cooker. Add the browned beef, halved apricots, beef broth, honey, cumin, coriander, cinnamon, and orange zest.

5. Stir everything together to ensure the ingredients are well combined. Cover the slow cooker and let it cook on low for 6-8 hours, or until the beef is tender and easy to shred.

6. Toast the slivered almonds in a dry skillet over medium heat for a few minutes, until golden and fragrant.

7. Once the stew is ready, garnish it with the toasted almonds just before serving.

---

## Slow Cooker Beef and Cherry Stew with Red Wine and Dark Chocolate

Servings: Two Portions
Prep Time: 20 minutes
Cook Time: 6-8 hours on low

### Ingredients:

- 1/2 lb beef stew meat (chuck), cut into 1-inch cubes
- 1/4 cup dried tart cherries
- 1/4 cup dry red wine (like Pinot Noir or Merlot)
- 1/2 cup low-sodium beef broth
- 1/2 small red onion, finely chopped
- 1/2 medium carrot, peeled and sliced
- 1/2 celery stalk, chopped
- 1/2 tablespoon tomato paste
- 1/2 teaspoon dried thyme
- 1 bay leaf
- 1/2 oz dark chocolate (70% cacao or higher), chopped finely
- 1/2 tablespoon olive oil
- 1/4 teaspoon balsamic vinegar
- Salt and freshly ground black pepper, to taste

### Instructions:

1. Pat the beef pieces dry with paper towels and season them generously with salt and freshly ground black pepper.

2. In a skillet, heat the olive oil over medium-high heat. Add the beef in batches and brown on all sides. Remove from the pan once browned and set aside.

3. In the same skillet, add the chopped onion, sliced carrot, and chopped celery. Cook for about 5 minutes, until they soften.

4. Transfer the sautéed vegetables to the slow cooker. Add the browned beef, dried cherries, red wine, beef broth, tomato paste, thyme, bay leaf, and balsamic vinegar.

5. Stir the ingredients together to mix well. Cover the slow cooker and cook on low for 6-8 hours, or until the beef is tender and cooked through.

6. Once done, remove the bay leaf and stir in the finely chopped dark chocolate. Let the chocolate melt completely and blend into the sauce.

7. Serve hot and enjoy the rich and hearty stew.

## Slow Cooker Balsamic Beef with Sweet Potatoes and Rosemary

Servings: Two Portions
Prep Time: 15 minutes
Cook Time: 4-6 hours on low

**Ingredients:**
- 1 lb beef stew meat (such as round or sirloin tip), cut into 1-inch cubes
- 1 medium sweet potato, peeled and diced into small pieces
- ¼ cup balsamic vinegar
- 1 cup low-sodium beef broth
- 1 small red onion, finely chopped
- 2 sprigs fresh rosemary
- 1 tablespoon pure maple syrup
- 1 tablespoon olive oil
- Salt and freshly ground black pepper, to taste
- ¼ teaspoon red pepper flakes (optional, for mild heat)

**Instructions:**
1. Pat the beef dry with a paper towel, then season generously with salt and black pepper.
2. Heat olive oil in a skillet over medium-high heat. Sear the beef in batches until evenly browned, then transfer to the slow cooker.
3. In the slow cooker, combine the diced sweet potatoes, chopped red onion, balsamic vinegar, beef broth, rosemary sprigs, and maple syrup. Stir to mix.
4. Add the seared beef to the slow cooker, ensuring it is well distributed.
5. Cover and cook on low for 4 to 6 hours, or until the beef is tender and the sweet potatoes are fork-soft.

6.  Discard the rosemary sprigs before serving. Taste and adjust seasoning as needed.

---

# Slow Cooker Pork Tenderloin with Apple-Cranberry Sauce

Portion Size: Serves two
Prep Time: 15 minutes
Cook Time: 3-4 hours on low

## Ingredients:

- 1 lb pork tenderloin, trimmed of excess silver skin
- 1 large apple (such as Honeycrisp or Gala), cored and chopped
- 1 cup fresh or frozen cranberries
- ½ cup apple cider or apple juice
- 2 tablespoons honey
- 1 tablespoon Dijon mustard
- ½ teaspoon ground cinnamon
- ¼ teaspoon ground cloves (adds warmth and depth)
- Salt and freshly ground black pepper, to taste

## Instructions:

1. Generously season the pork tenderloin with salt and black pepper.

2. In the slow cooker, mix the chopped apple, cranberries, apple cider, honey, Dijon mustard, cinnamon, and ground cloves.

3. Place the seasoned pork tenderloin on top of the fruit mixture.

4. Cover and cook on low for 3-4 hours, or until the pork reaches an internal temperature of 145°F (63°C). Use a meat thermometer for accuracy.

5. Once done, remove the pork from the slow cooker and rest for 5-10 minutes. This helps the juices redistribute, making the meat more tender and flavorful.

6. Slice the pork and serve with the apple-cranberry sauce from the slow cooker.

# Slow Cooker Pulled Pork with Peach-Bourbon BBQ Sauce

Servings: Two portions
Prep Time: 20 minutes
Cook Time: 6-8 hours on low

## Ingredients:

- ¾ lb pork shoulder, trimmed of excess fat
- 1 (15-ounce) can of sliced peaches in light syrup, drained (reserve ½ cup syrup)
- ¼ cup bourbon (or substitute with apple juice or extra peach syrup)
- 2 tablespoons apple cider vinegar
- 1 tablespoon packed light brown sugar
- 1 tablespoon smoked paprika
- 1 teaspoon chili powder
- ½ teaspoon garlic powder
- ¼ teaspoon cayenne pepper (optional, for a hint of heat)
- Salt and freshly ground black pepper, to taste

## Instructions:

1. Generously season the pork shoulder with salt and black pepper.
2. In the slow cooker, mix the reserved peach syrup, bourbon (or apple juice), apple cider vinegar, brown sugar, smoked paprika, chili powder, garlic powder, and cayenne pepper (if using).
3. Place the seasoned pork into the sauce mixture, making sure it's well coated.
4. Cover and cook on low for 6-8 hours, until the meat becomes tender and shreds effortlessly with a fork.
5. Once done, remove the pork and use two forks to shred it into smaller pieces.
6. Skim off any excess fat from the sauce left in the slow cooker.
7. Return the shredded pork to the slow cooker and mix it with the sauce for extra flavor.
8. Serve hot, either in sandwiches or over rice or potatoes.

# Slow Cooker Pork & Sweet Potato Curry with Coconut Milk

Servings: 2 perfectly portioned meals
Prep Time: 15 minutes
Cook Time: 4-6 hours on low

## Ingredients:

- ¾ lb pork tenderloin or boneless pork loin cut into 1-inch cubes
- 1 medium sweet potato, peeled and diced into ½-inch chunks
- 1 cup full-fat coconut milk (rich and creamy)
- 1 small yellow onion, finely chopped
- 1-inch piece of fresh ginger, grated
- 1 tablespoon high-quality curry powder
- ½ teaspoon ground cumin
- ¼ teaspoon ground turmeric
- 1 tablespoon honey or maple syrup (for a subtle sweetness)
- Juice of ½ lime (stirred in at the end for freshness)
- Salt and freshly ground black pepper, to taste

## Instructions:

1. Season the pork pieces generously with salt and black pepper.
2. In the slow cooker, mix the diced sweet potato, coconut milk, chopped onion, grated ginger, curry powder, cumin, turmeric, and honey (or maple syrup).
3. Add the seasoned pork, ensuring everything is well coated.
4. Cover and cook on low for 4-6 hours, until the pork is tender and the sweet potato is soft.
5. Right before serving, stir in the lime juice to enhance the flavors.

## Slow Cooker Pork with Pineapple and Peppers

Servings: Makes just enough for two, ideal over rice or noodles.
Prep Time: 15 minutes
Cook Time: 4-6 hours on low

### Ingredients:

- ¾ lb pork tenderloin or boneless pork loin, cut into bite-sized pieces
- 1 cup pineapple chunks (fresh or canned in juice), drained
- ¼ cup reserved pineapple juice
- 1 red bell pepper, chopped
- 1 green bell pepper, chopped
- ¼ cup low-sodium soy sauce or tamari
- 1 tablespoon brown sugar
- 1 tablespoon rice vinegar
- 1 teaspoon ground ginger
- 2 cloves garlic, minced
- ½ teaspoon red pepper flakes (optional, for spice)
- Cooked rice or noodles (for serving)
- Salt and black pepper to taste

### Instructions:

1. Season the Pork: Sprinkle the pork pieces with salt and black pepper.
2. Prepare the Sauce: In the slow cooker, mix the reserved pineapple juice, soy sauce, brown sugar, rice vinegar, ginger, garlic, and red pepper flakes (if using).
3. Assemble in Slow Cooker: Add the pork pieces and chopped bell peppers to the sauce, stirring to coat everything evenly.
4. Cook Slowly: Cover and let it cook on low for 4-6 hours until the pork is tender and infused with flavor.

5. Serve & Enjoy: Spoon the pork and sauce over freshly cooked rice or noodles.

---

# Slow Cooker Honey Mustard Pork with Roasted Root Vegetables

Servings: Two Portions
Prep Time: 25 minutes (includes roasting vegetables)
Cook Time: 3-4 hours on low

## Ingredients

- **For the Pork:**
  - 1 lb pork tenderloin, trimmed of excess fat
  - 1 tbsp olive oil
  - Salt and freshly ground black pepper
  - For the Honey Mustard Glaze:
  - 2 tbsp Dijon mustard
  - 2 tbsp honey
  - 1 tbsp apple cider vinegar
  - ½ tsp dried thyme
  - ¼ tsp ground allspice
- **For the Roasted Vegetables:**
  - 1 medium carrot, peeled and chopped
  - 1 medium parsnip, peeled and chopped
  - 1 small red potato, quartered
  - 1 small apple, cored and chopped
  - 1 tbsp olive oil
  - Salt and freshly ground black pepper

## Instructions

1. Preheat & Roast the Vegetables: Preheat the oven to 400°F (200°C). On a baking sheet, toss the carrot, parsnip, potato, and apple with olive oil, salt, and black pepper. Roast for 20-25 minutes until they are tender and slightly caramelized.

2. Season the Pork: While the vegetables roast, pat the pork tenderloin dry and season generously with salt and black pepper.

3. Prepare the Glaze: In the slow cooker, whisk together Dijon mustard, honey, apple cider vinegar, thyme, and allspice until well combined.

4. Cook the Pork: Place the seasoned pork tenderloin into the slow cooker, coating it in the honey mustard glaze. Cover and cook on low for 3-4 hours or until the pork reaches an internal temperature of 145°F (63°C).

5. Rest & Slice: Once done, remove the pork from the slow cooker and let it rest for 5-10 minutes before slicing.

6. Serve: Plate the sliced pork alongside the roasted root vegetables and apple. Drizzle the reserved glaze from the slow cooker over the top for extra flavor.

---

# CHAPTER SEVEN: DESSERTS RECIPES

## Slow Cooker Apple Cinnamon Bread Pudding (Small-Batch)

Servings: Two Portions
Prep Time: 15 minutes
Cook Time: 2-3 hours on low

### Ingredients:
- 4 slices day-old challah or brioche, cut into 1-inch cubes
- 1 medium apple (Honeycrisp or Gala), peeled, cored, and diced
- 1 cup whole or 2% milk (for creaminess)
- 2 large eggs
- 2 tbsp maple syrup
- 1 tsp ground cinnamon
- ½ tsp vanilla extract
- A pinch of salt
- 1 tbsp unsalted butter, melted

### Instructions:
1. Prepare the Dish: Lightly grease a small oven-safe dish (around 5x7 inches) that fits inside your slow cooker.
2. Make the Custard: In a medium bowl, whisk together milk, eggs, maple syrup, cinnamon, vanilla, and salt until fully .
3. Soak the Bread: Add the cubed bread and diced apple to the custard mixture. Gently stir to coat all pieces evenly.
4. Assemble in Slow Cooker: Transfer the mixture into the greased dish. Drizzle the melted butter evenly over the top.
5. Cook: Place the dish inside the slow cooker, cover, and cook on low for 2-3 hours. The pudding is done when the center is set and a knife inserted comes out mostly clean.
6. Cool & Serve: Allow the pudding to cool slightly before serving warm.

# Slow Cooker Chocolate Peanut Butter Swirl Brownies

Servings: Two Portions
Prep Time: 15 minutes
Cook Time: 1.5-2 hours on low

## Ingredients:

- 3 tbsp unsalted butter, melted
- ⅓ cup granulated sugar
- 3 tbsp unsweetened cocoa powder
- ¼ tsp salt
- 1 large egg
- ½ tsp vanilla extract
- 3 tbsp all-purpose flour
- ¼ cup creamy peanut butter, melted

## Instructions:

1. Prepare the Baking Dish: Lightly grease a small oven-safe dish (around 5x5 inches) that fits inside your slow cooker—line with parchment paper for easy removal.

2. Mix the Batter: In a medium bowl, whisk together melted butter, sugar, cocoa powder, and salt until smooth.

3. Incorporate Wet Ingredients: Add egg and vanilla extract, whisking until fully combined.

4. Fold in Dry Ingredients: Gently stir in flour, mixing only until just combined—avoid overmixing for a fudgy texture.

5. Layer & Swirl: Pour half the brownie batter into the prepared dish. Drizzle with half the melted peanut butter. Repeat with the remaining batter and peanut butter, then use a knife or toothpick to swirl the layers together.

6. Cook in Slow Cooker: Place the dish inside the slow cooker. Cover with a clean kitchen towel or double-layer paper towel under the lid (this absorbs condensation). Cook on low for 1.5-2 hours or until a toothpick inserted near the edge comes out with moist crumbs (the center remains soft).

7. Cool & Serve: Let the brownies cool completely in the dish before cutting into two even portions.

# Slow Cooker Peach Cobbler for Two

Portioning: Makes two servings
Prep Time: 15 minutes
Cook Time: 2-3 hours on low

## Ingredients:
- 1 cup sliced peaches (fresh, or about 8 ounces canned peaches in light syrup, drained)
- 2 tablespoons reserved peach syrup/juice (or milk)
- ⅛ teaspoon ground cinnamon

## For the Topping:
- ⅓ cup all-purpose flour
- 3 tablespoons granulated sugar
- ¼ teaspoon baking powder
- Pinch of salt
- 2 tablespoons cold unsalted butter, cut into small pieces

## Instructions:
1. In the slow cooker, gently toss the sliced peaches with the cinnamon and reserved syrup/juice.
2. In a small bowl, whisk together the flour, sugar, baking powder, and salt.
3. Using a pastry blender or your fingertips, cut in the cold butter until the mixture forms coarse crumbs.
4. Stir in the peach syrup/milk until just combined to create a soft crumble.
5. Evenly sprinkle the topping over the peaches in the slow cooker.
6. Cover and cook on low for 2-3 hours, until the topping is lightly golden and the peaches are tender and bubbly.

# Slow Cooker Spiced Poached Pears for Two

Servings: 2 (four pear halves)
Prep Time: 10 minutes
Cook Time: 2-3 hours on low

## Ingredients:

- 2 firm yet ripe pears (like Bosc or Anjou), peeled, cored, and halved
- 1 cup apple juice or a dry white wine (such as Riesling)
- 2 tablespoons honey
- 1 cinnamon stick
- 2 whole cloves
- 1 star anise (optional)
- ¼ teaspoon freshly grated nutmeg

## Instructions:

1. Arrange Pears: Lay the pear halves in a single layer at the bottom of your slow cooker.

2. Prepare the Poaching Liquid: In a small bowl, blend the apple juice (or wine), honey, cinnamon stick, cloves, star anise (if using), and nutmeg. Pour this aromatic mixture over the pears.

3. Cook Gently: Cover the slow cooker and cook on low for 2-3 hours, until the pears are tender but still hold their shape. They should pierce easily with a fork.

4. Serve: Carefully lift the pears from the slow cooker, serving them warm with a drizzle of the spiced poaching liquid.

## Slow Cooker Banana "Nice" Cream for Two

Servings: 2
Prep Time: 5 minutes (plus freezing time)
Cook Time: 2-3 hours on low (for softening, not cooking)

### Ingredients:
- 2 ripe bananas, peeled, sliced into ½-inch rounds, and completely frozen
- ¼ cup unsweetened almond milk or preferred milk (dairy or non-dairy)
- 1 tablespoon creamy peanut butter (optional)
- ½ teaspoon vanilla extract (optional)
- Small pinch of salt (optional, to enhance sweetness)

### Instructions:
1. Soften the Bananas: Place the frozen banana slices in the slow cooker and pour in the milk.
2. Slow Heat: Cover and set to low for 2-3 hours, checking periodically. The bananas should be soft to blend but not melted or overly mushy.
3. Blend Until Creamy: Transfer the softened bananas to a blender or food processor. Add peanut butter, vanilla, and salt (if using). Blend until smooth, scraping down the sides as needed.
4. Serve Immediately or Freeze: Enjoy right away for a soft-serve texture, or freeze for 30-60 minutes for a firmer consistency.

# Slow Cooker Cranberry Orange Cobbler for Two

Servings: 2
Prep Time: 15 minutes
Cook Time: 2-2.5 hours on low

## Ingredients:

- **Filling:**
  - 1 cup fresh or frozen cranberries
  - ½ medium orange, zested and juiced (about 2 tbsp juice)
  - 2 tbsp maple syrup (adjust for sweetness)
  - ¼ tsp ground ginger

- **Topping:**
  - ½ cup rolled oats (not instant)
  - 2 tbsp almond flour
  - 2 tbsp light brown sugar, packed
  - ¼ tsp ground cinnamon
  - 2 tbsp melted coconut oil

## Instructions:

1. Prepare the Filling: In the slow cooker, mix cranberries, orange zest, orange juice, maple syrup, and ground ginger. Stir gently to coat the fruit.
2. Make the Topping: In a bowl, combine oats, almond flour, brown sugar, and cinnamon. Stir in melted coconut oil until the mixture becomes crumbly.
3. Assemble & Cook: Evenly sprinkle the topping over the cranberry mixture. Cover and cook on low for 2-2.5 hours, until the cranberries are soft and bubbling, and the topping is golden and slightly chewy.

# Slow Cooker Mini Chocolate Lava Cakes with Raspberry Sauce

Servings: Two Portions
Prep Time: 10 minutes
Cook Time: 1-1.5 hours on low

## Ingredients:
- For the Lava Cakes:
- 2 oz bittersweet chocolate (70% cacao), finely chopped
- 2 tbsp unsalted butter
- ¼ cup granulated sugar
- 1 large egg yolk
- ¼ tsp vanilla extract
- Pinch of salt

## For the Raspberry Sauce:
- ½ cup fresh or frozen raspberries
- 1 tbsp granulated sugar
- 1 tsp fresh lemon juice

## Instructions:
1. Prepare the Ramekins: Lightly grease two small (4-oz) ramekins.
2. Melt the Chocolate: In a heatproof bowl, melt the chopped chocolate and butter together using a double boiler or short microwave bursts, stirring until smooth. Avoid overheating.
3. Mix the Batter: In a separate bowl, whisk sugar and egg yolk until pale and slightly thick. Gradually add the melted chocolate mixture, stirring until well incorporated. Mix in the vanilla extract and salt.
4. Fill the Ramekins: Divide the batter evenly between the ramekins.
5. Slow Cook: Place the ramekins in the slow cooker. Cover with a clean towel or paper towel under the lid to absorb condensation. Cook on low for 1-1.5 hours, until the edges are set but the center remains soft. The cakes should jiggle slightly in the middle when gently shaken.

6. Prepare the Raspberry Sauce: While the cakes cook, heat raspberries, sugar, and lemon juice in a small saucepan over low heat. Mash gently and simmer until thickened (5-7 minutes). Strain to remove seeds if desired.

7. Serve Immediately: Carefully remove the ramekins from the slow cooker and serve warm, drizzled with raspberry sauce.

## Slow Cooker Lemon Blueberry Grunt for Two

Portions: Makes enough for two
Prep Time: 15 minutes
Cook Time: 1.5-2 hours on low

### Ingredients

- **Blueberry Base:**
    - 3/4 cup fresh or frozen blueberries
    - Zest of half a medium lemon
    - 1 tablespoon lemon juice
    - 1 tablespoon sugar

- **Biscuit Topping:**
    - 1/3 cup all-purpose flour
    - 1 tablespoon sugar
    - 1/2 teaspoon baking powder
    - Pinch of salt
    - 2 tablespoons cold, unsalted butter, cut into small pieces
    - 1 1/2 to 2 tablespoons milk (whole or 2%)

### Instructions

1. Prepare the Blueberries:
   In your slow cooker, mix the blueberries with the lemon zest, lemon juice, and sugar until well coated.
2. Make the Biscuit Dough:
   In a bowl, combine flour, sugar, baking powder, and a pinch of salt. Cut in the cold butter using your fingers or a pastry cutter until the mixture resembles coarse crumbs. Add 1 1/2 tablespoons of milk and mix gently, adding more milk if needed, just until the dough comes together—avoid overmixing.
3. Assemble in the Slow Cooker:
   Drop small spoonfuls of the biscuit dough (around 4-5 mounds) evenly over the blueberry mixture in the slow cooker.

4. Cook Until Golden:
   Cover and set to low. Cook for 1.5 to 2 hours, or until the biscuit topping is firm and lightly golden, and the blueberries are bubbling.

---

# Slow Cooker Chai-Infused Pears with Honey Yogurt

Servings: 2 (Four pear halves)
Prep Time: 10 minutes
Cook Time: 2-3 hours on low

## Ingredients
- 2 firm pears (such as Bosc or Anjou), peeled, cored, and cut in half
- ¾ cup apple cider or white grape juice
- 1 ½ tablespoons honey
- 1 chai tea bag (or a mix of ¼ teaspoon each of cinnamon, ginger, and cardamom, plus a pinch of cloves and black pepper)
- For topping: ⅓ cup plain Greek yogurt, extra honey for drizzling (optional), and chopped nuts (optional)

## Instructions
1. Prepare the Pears: Place the pear halves in a single layer inside the slow cooker.
2. Mix the Spices: If using a chai tea bag, cut it open and mix the contents with apple cider and honey. If using individual spices, stir them into the liquid. Pour the mixture over the pears.
3. Slow Cook: Cover with the lid and cook on low for 2-3 hours, or until the pears become soft but still hold their shape.
4. Serve: Let the pears cool slightly before serving. Top each half with a spoonful of Greek yogurt, drizzle with honey, and sprinkle with chopped nuts if desired.

---

# Slow Cooker Sweet Potato Pudding with Crunchy Pecan Topping

Servings: Two Portions
Prep Time: 15 minutes
Cook Time: 2-3 hours on low + 30 minutes uncovered

## Ingredients:

- **For the Pudding:**
    - 1 small sweet potato (6-7 oz), peeled and diced into ½-inch cubes
    - ⅓ cup whole milk (or almond milk)
    - 1 ½ tablespoons maple syrup
    - ⅜ teaspoon cinnamon (just under ½ teaspoon)
    - ⅛ teaspoon nutmeg
    - Small pinch of salt

- **For the Topping:**
    - 3 tablespoons chopped pecans
    - 1 ½ tablespoons rolled oats
    - 2 teaspoons packed brown sugar
    - 2 teaspoons melted butter or coconut oil

## Instructions:

1. Prepare the Base: Place the sweet potato cubes into the slow cooker. Pour in the milk, add the maple syrup, cinnamon, nutmeg, and salt, then mix everything.

2. Slow Cook: Cover with the lid and cook on low for 2-3 hours, or until the sweet potatoes are tender enough to mash.

3. Mash the Sweet Potatoes: Use a fork or a masher to mash the sweet potatoes until mostly smooth, leaving some texture if preferred.

4. Make the Topping: In a small bowl, mix the chopped pecans, oats, brown sugar, and melted butter (or coconut oil) until the mixture becomes crumbly.

5. Add the Topping: Spread the pecan mixture evenly over the mashed sweet potatoes.

6. Finish Cooking: Remove the lid and continue cooking on low for another 30 minutes, allowing the topping to crisp up slightly. Keep an eye on it to prevent burning.

7. Serve and Enjoy: Scoop the pudding into bowls and serve warm.

# CHAPTER EIGHT: VEGAN RECIPES

## Slow Cooker Chickpea and Spinach Stew with Coconut Milk

Servings: Two Portions
Prep Time: 15 minutes
Cook Time: 4-6 hours on low

**Ingredients:**
- **Base Ingredients:**
  - 1 (15-ounce) can chickpeas, drained and rinsed
  - 4 ounces fresh spinach, chopped
  - 1 cup full-fat coconut milk (about half a standard 14-ounce can)
  - ½ small onion, finely chopped
  - 1 clove garlic, minced
  - ½-inch piece of fresh ginger, grated

- **Seasonings & Spices:**
  - 2 teaspoons curry powder
  - ¼ teaspoon ground cumin
  - ⅛ teaspoon turmeric
  - ⅛ teaspoon red pepper flakes (optional, for heat)
  - ¼ teaspoon garam masala (stirred in at the end)
  - Salt and black pepper, to taste
  - 2 teaspoons fresh lime juice (added at the end)

**Instructions**

1. Prepare the Base: Place the chickpeas, spinach, coconut milk, onion, garlic, ginger, curry powder, cumin, turmeric, and red pepper flakes (if using) into the slow cooker—season with salt and black pepper.
2. Cook Slowly: Stir everything together, cover, and let it cook on low for 4-6 hours, allowing the flavors to blend and the spinach to soften.
3. Finish & Serve: Just before serving, mix in the garam masala and fresh lime juice for added flavor. Serve warm.

# Slow Cooker Hearty Lentil Soup with Roasted Veggies & Balsamic Swirl

Servings: 2 filling bowl
Prep Time: 20 minutes (includes roasting time)
Cook Time: 4-6 hours on low

## Ingredients

- **For the Soup:**
  - ¾ cup dried green or brown lentils, rinsed
  - 3 cups vegetable broth (low-sodium recommended)
  - 1 small carrot, peeled and chopped
  - 1 small parsnip, peeled and diced
  - ½ red bell pepper, cut into small pieces
  - ½ small red onion, finely diced

- **For Seasoning:**
  - 1 tablespoon olive oil
  - ¾ teaspoon dried thyme
  - ¼ teaspoon smoked paprika
  - Salt and black pepper, to taste
  - 1½ tablespoons balsamic vinegar

## Instructions:

1. Roast the Vegetables: Preheat the oven to 400°F (200°C). In a bowl, toss the chopped carrot, parsnip, bell pepper, and onion with olive oil, a pinch of salt, and black pepper. Spread them evenly on a baking sheet and roast for 15-20 minutes, stirring once, until they develop a golden color and slightly caramelized edges.

2. Assemble in the Slow Cooker: Transfer the roasted vegetables into the slow cooker. Add the rinsed lentils, vegetable broth, thyme, and smoked paprika. Give everything a good stir, then season with salt and pepper to your taste.

3. Let It Simmer: Cover and cook on low for 4-6 hours, or until the lentils soften and absorb all the flavors.

4. Prepare the Balsamic Drizzle: While the soup is cooking, pour the balsamic vinegar into a small saucepan. Heat it over medium heat, stirring occasionally, until it thickens slightly into a glaze (about 5-7 minutes). Keep an eye on it to prevent burning.
5. Serve & Enjoy: Pour the hot soup into bowls and finish with a drizzle of balsamic reduction. Serve immediately and enjoy its deep, savory flavors.

# Slow Cooker Creamy Butternut Squash & Apple Risotto for Two

Servings: 2 satisfying portions
Prep Time: 15 minutes
Cook Time: 2-3 hours on low

## Ingredients:

- ½ small butternut squash (about ½ pound), peeled, seeded, and diced into small cubes
- ½ medium apple (such as Honeycrisp or Gala), peeled, cored, and chopped
- 2 cups vegetable broth, warmed
- ⅓ cup Arborio rice
- 3 tablespoons grated Parmesan cheese (plus extra for garnish)
- 1 teaspoon unsalted butter
- ½ small shallot, finely minced
- ¼ teaspoon fresh sage, finely chopped (or a pinch of dried)
- Salt and black pepper to taste

## Instructions

1. Melt the butter in a pan over medium heat. Add the minced shallot and cook for about 2-3 minutes until soft and fragrant.
2. Transfer the shallot to the slow cooker, then add the diced butternut squash, chopped apple, and warmed vegetable broth. Stir everything together.
3. Cover and cook on low for about 1.5 to 2 hours, or until the squash becomes tender.
4. Stir in the Arborio rice, cover again, and continue cooking for another 30-45 minutes, stirring occasionally. If the risotto thickens too much, add a little extra warm broth, one tablespoon at a time, until it reaches a creamy consistency.
5. Once the rice is fully cooked and creamy, stir in the Parmesan cheese and chopped sage. Season with salt and black pepper to taste.
6. Serve warm, garnished with extra Parmesan cheese if desired.

## Slow Cooker Spiced Sweet Potato and Black Bean Chili

Servings: Perfectly portioned for two
Prep Time: 15 minutes
Cook Time: 4-6 hours on low

**Ingredients:**

- 1 medium sweet potato (about ½ pound), peeled and cut into bite-sized cubes
- 1 can (15 ounces) black beans, drained and rinsed
- 1 can (14.5 ounces) diced tomatoes, including their juices
- 1 small onion, finely chopped
- 1 bell pepper (any color), diced
- 2 cloves garlic, minced
- 1 tablespoon chili seasoning blend
- 1 teaspoon ground cumin
- ½ teaspoon smoked paprika
- ¼ teaspoon cayenne pepper (optional, for a spicy kick)
- ½ teaspoon dried oregano
- Salt and black pepper, to taste
- 1 tablespoon fresh lime juice (stirred in at the end)
- Optional toppings: fresh cilantro, shredded cheese, sour cream, or Greek yogurt

**Instructions:**

1. Add the sweet potato cubes, black beans, diced tomatoes with juices, chopped onion, diced bell pepper, and minced garlic to the slow cooker.

2. Sprinkle in the chili seasoning, cumin, smoked paprika, cayenne (if using), and oregano. Season with salt and black pepper.

3. Stir the ingredients to evenly distribute the flavors. Cover the slow cooker and cook on low for 4 to 6 hours, or until the sweet potatoes are fork-tender.

4. Just before serving, stir in the fresh lime juice for a burst of brightness.

5. Dish into bowls and top with your favorite garnishes like fresh cilantro, shredded cheese, or a dollop of sour cream or Greek yogurt.

# Slow Cooker Eggplant Parmesan for Two

Servings: 2 individual portions
Prep Time: 20 minutes (plus 30 minutes for salting)
Cook Time: 2–3 hours on low

## Ingredients

- 1 medium eggplant (about 1 pound), sliced into ½-inch rounds
- 1 teaspoon salt (for draining excess moisture)
- 2 tablespoons olive oil, divided
- 1 cup crushed tomatoes
- 1 small onion, finely chopped
- 2 cloves garlic, minced
- 1 teaspoon dried oregano
- ⅓ cup shredded mozzarella cheese
- 3 tablespoons grated Parmesan cheese
- Fresh basil, for garnish (optional)
- Salt and freshly ground black pepper, to taste

## Instructions

1. Remove Excess Moisture: Arrange the eggplant slices on a paper towel-lined tray. Sprinkle with salt and let them sit for 30 minutes to draw out moisture. Afterward, pat them dry thoroughly to prevent sogginess.
2. Brown the Eggplant: Heat 1 tablespoon of olive oil in a pan over medium heat. Sear the eggplant slices in batches for 2–3 minutes per side until lightly golden. Set aside.
3. Make the Sauce: In the same pan, add the remaining tablespoon of olive oil. Sauté the chopped onion and garlic until softened, about 5 minutes. Stir in the crushed tomatoes, dried oregano, salt, and black pepper. Let the sauce simmer for a couple of minutes.
4. Assemble in the Slow Cooker: Spread a thin layer of sauce on the bottom of the slow cooker. Arrange half of the eggplant slices over the sauce, followed by half of the mozzarella and Parmesan. Repeat the layers with the remaining ingredients.

5. Slow Cook: Cover and cook on low for 2–3 hours, until the eggplant is fork-tender and the cheese is melted.

6. Serve: Let it rest for a few minutes before serving. Garnish with fresh basil if desired.

---

## Slow Cooker Creamy Tomato and White Bean Soup with Pesto Drizzle

Servings: 2 generous bowls
Prep Time: 15 minutes
Cook Time: 4–6 hours on low

### Ingredients
- 1 (14-ounce) can crushed tomatoes
- 1 (7.5-ounce) can cannellini beans, rinsed and drained
- 1 small yellow onion, finely chopped
- 2 cloves garlic, minced
- ½ teaspoon dried basil
- ¼ teaspoon dried oregano
- 3 tablespoons heavy cream (or full-fat coconut milk for a vegan option)
- Salt and freshly ground black pepper, to taste

### For the Pesto Drizzle
- ¼ cup fresh basil leaves, packed
- 1 tablespoon grated Parmesan (or nutritional yeast for a vegan version)
- 1 tablespoon toasted pine nuts or walnuts
- 1 small garlic clove
- 1½ tablespoons extra virgin olive oil
- Pinch of salt

### Instructions
1. Prepare the Soup Base: In the slow cooker, combine the crushed tomatoes, cannellini beans, chopped onion, minced garlic, dried basil, and dried oregano. Season with salt and black pepper.
2. Cook Low and Slow: Cover and cook on low for 4–6 hours, allowing the flavors to deepen.
3. Make the Pesto: While the soup simmers, blend basil leaves, Parmesan (or nutritional yeast), toasted nuts, garlic, olive oil, and a pinch of salt in a food processor until smooth. Scrape the sides as needed.

4. Finish the Soup: Just before serving, stir in the heavy cream or coconut milk to add richness.
5. Serve: Ladle the soup into bowls and swirl a spoonful of pesto into each. Enjoy immediately.

# Slow Cooker Quinoa and Vegetable Curry with Mango Chutney

Servings: 2 portions
Prep Time: 20 minutes
Cook Time: 2–3 hours on low

## Ingredients

- ½ cup quinoa, rinsed
- 1 cup low-sodium vegetable broth
- 1 cup mixed vegetables (such as cauliflower, broccoli, carrots, and peas), cut into small pieces
- 1 small yellow onion, finely diced
- 2 cloves garlic, minced
- 1-inch piece fresh ginger, grated
- 1 tablespoon curry powder (use a high-quality blend)
- ½ teaspoon ground cumin
- ¼ teaspoon turmeric
- ¼ teaspoon crushed red pepper flakes (optional, for spice)
- Salt and freshly ground black pepper, to taste
- 2 tablespoons mango chutney (for serving)
- Fresh cilantro or parsley, for garnish (optional)

## Instructions

1. Prepare the Base: Place the rinsed quinoa into the slow cooker. Add the vegetable broth, chopped vegetables, diced onion, minced garlic, and grated ginger.

2. Season the Dish: Sprinkle in the curry powder, cumin, turmeric, and crushed red pepper flakes (if using). Add salt and black pepper to taste, then stir everything together until well combined.

3. Cook Until Tender: Cover the slow cooker and set it to low. Let the curry cook for 2–3 hours, or until the quinoa is fluffy and the vegetables are soft. The liquid should be fully absorbed.

4. Serve and Garnish: Spoon the curry into bowls while warm. Add a spoonful of mango chutney on top for a sweet contrast, and sprinkle with fresh cilantro or parsley if desired.

# Slow Cooker Vegetarian Stuffed Peppers

Servings: 2 stuffed peppers (ideal for two people)
Prep Time: 25 minutes
Cook Time: 3–4 hours on low

## Ingredients:

- 2 large bell peppers (any color), sliced in half lengthwise and seeds removed
- 1 cup cooked brown rice or quinoa
- 1 (14.5-ounce) can diced tomatoes, drained
- ½ cup black beans or corn (or a mix of both)
- ½ cup finely chopped onion
- 1 garlic clove, minced
- 1 teaspoon dried oregano
- ½ teaspoon dried basil
- ¼ cup shredded cheddar or Monterey Jack cheese (optional, or use nutritional yeast for a dairy-free option)
- 1 tablespoon olive oil
- Salt and freshly ground black pepper, to taste

## Instructions:

1. Make the Filling: In a mixing bowl, combine the cooked rice or quinoa with the drained diced tomatoes, black beans or corn, chopped onion, minced garlic, oregano, basil, olive oil, salt, and black pepper. Stir everything together until well mixed.

2. Fill the Peppers: Spoon the mixture evenly into the four bell pepper halves, pressing lightly to pack the filling.

3. Slow Cook: Arrange the stuffed peppers in the slow cooker, and cut side up. Add ½ cup of water to the bottom to create steam, which helps the peppers cook evenly. Cover and cook on low for 3–4 hours, or until the peppers are soft.

4. Add Cheese (Optional): If using cheese or nutritional yeast, sprinkle it over the stuffed peppers during the last 30 minutes of cooking. For a crispier

top, transfer the peppers to a baking sheet and broil for a few minutes before serving.

---

# Slow Cooker Creamy Spinach and Artichoke Dip

Servings: Make two individual portions
Prep Time: 10 minutes
Cook Time: 1.5–2 hours on low

## Ingredients:

- 4 ounces cream cheese, softened
- ¼ cup sour cream or plain Greek yogurt
- ½ cup frozen spinach, thawed and well-drained
- 1 (14-ounce) can artichoke hearts, drained and finely chopped (not marinated)
- ¼ cup grated Parmesan cheese (or nutritional yeast for a dairy-free option)
- 2 tablespoons mayonnaise (or vegan mayo for a plant-based version)
- 1 garlic clove, finely minced
- ¼ teaspoon red pepper flakes (optional, for a bit of spice)
- Salt and freshly ground black pepper, to taste
- A pinch of nutmeg for extra depth
- Tortilla chips, pita bread, or toasted baguette slices for dipping

## Instructions:

1. Prepare the Mixture: In a mixing bowl, combine the softened cream cheese, sour cream (or Greek yogurt), well-drained spinach, chopped artichoke hearts, Parmesan (or nutritional yeast), mayonnaise, minced garlic, red pepper flakes (if using), salt, black pepper, and nutmeg. Stir until everything is well blended.

2. Divide into Portions: Spoon the mixture evenly into two small, oven-safe ramekins that fit inside your slow cooker.

3. Slow Cook: Arrange the ramekins inside the slow cooker, cover with the lid, and cook on low for 1.5–2 hours, or until the dip is heated through, bubbling around the edges, and the cheese is fully melted.

4. Serve Warm: Enjoy the dip straight from the ramekins with tortilla chips, pita bread, or toasted baguette slices.

# Slow Cooker Maple-Glazed Carrots with Pecans and Cranberries

Servings: Two side portions
Prep Time: 10 minutes
Cook Time: 2–3 hours on low

## Ingredients

- ½ pound carrots, peeled and sliced into ½-inch rounds
- 1 tablespoon pure maple syrup
- ½ tablespoon butter or olive oil
- 2 tablespoons dried cranberries
- 2 tablespoons chopped pecans, toasted (toasting enhances crunch and flavor)
- ⅛ teaspoon ground cinnamon
- A small pinch of salt
- A tiny pinch of freshly grated nutmeg (optional, for warmth)

## Instructions:

1. Prepare  the Carrots: Place the sliced carrots in the slow cooker. Drizzle them with maple syrup, add the butter or olive oil, and sprinkle with cinnamon and salt. Stir everything together to coat the carrots evenly.
2. Cook on Low: Cover and set the slow cooker to low heat for 2–3 hours until the carrots are tender but still hold their shape.
3. Toast the Pecans: While the carrots are cooking, toast the chopped pecans in a dry pan over medium heat for 2–3 minutes, stirring frequently, until golden and fragrant. Keep an eye on them to prevent burning.
4. Add the Mix-ins: About 30 minutes before the cooking time is up, stir in the toasted pecans and dried cranberries.
5. Serve Warm: Once done, gently stir everything together and serve immediately.

# CHAPTER NINE: PREMIUM TIPS

## Tips and Tricks for Using a Slow Cooker Effectively

A slow cooker is a versatile and convenient kitchen tool that simplifies cooking while producing rich, flavorful meals. To ensure you're maximizing the potential of your slow cooker, consider these helpful tips and tricks.

1. Layer Your Ingredients Correctly

To ensure even cooking, layer your ingredients in the correct order. Denser items, such as root vegetables (e.g., carrots, potatoes) or meats, should go at the bottom of the slow cooker. These ingredients require more time to cook and benefit from direct heat. Lighter vegetables and delicate items should be placed on top, as they cook faster and don't need as much heat. This arrangement ensures everything cooks at the optimal temperature and prevents overcooking.

2. Avoid Lifting the Lid

It's tempting to check on your food while it's cooking, but each time you lift the lid, you let the heat escape. This drop in temperature can extend the cooking time and cause uneven cooking. Slow cookers are designed to retain heat, so keep the lid on as much as possible. If you do need to check the progress, do so quickly and avoid removing the lid for long.

3. Use the Right Size Slow Cooker

Using the correct size slow cooker is essential for optimal results. A slow cooker that's too large for the amount of food can cause food to dry out or cook too quickly. Conversely, using a small cooker for larger portions may lead to undercooking or spillage. A 3- to 4-quart slow cooker is ideal for smaller meals (e.g., for one or two people), while a 6-quart slow cooker is better suited for larger batches.

## 4. Brown Your Meat First

Although optional, browning meats before adding them to the slow cooker enhances the flavor of your dish. Browning creates a layer of caramelization that adds richness and depth to the taste. Simply heat a pan with a little oil, brown the meat on all sides, then transfer it to the slow cooker. This extra step will elevate the overall flavor of your meal.

## 5. Adjust Cooking Times for Different Models

Not all slow cookers are the same, and their cooking times can vary. Some models cook faster or slower than others, and older models may take longer. If you're using a new slow cooker, you may need to reduce the cooking time slightly. Monitor your dish the first time you use a new cooker and adjust accordingly. Typically, cooking on low takes about 6-8 hours, while cooking on high takes about 3-4 hours.

## 6. Season Gradually

It's easy to over-season a dish, especially in a slow cooker. As food simmers, flavors intensify. To control seasoning, it's best to start with a base level of seasoning and adjust towards the end of cooking. Taste the dish in the final stages and add salt, pepper, or herbs to your preference. This method helps prevent over-seasoning and gives you more control over the final flavor.

## 7. Add Dairy at the End

If your recipe includes dairy (such as cream, milk, or cheese), it's best to add it at the end of the cooking process. Dairy can curdle or break down if cooked for too long, especially on high heat. Stir in dairy products during the last 30 minutes of cooking to ensure they stay creamy and smooth.

# Handling Leftovers with Ease

Slow cookers are perfect for preparing larger portions, and inevitably, there will be leftovers. Properly storing and using these leftovers can help you reduce food waste and maximize the value of your meals. Here are some useful tips for handling leftovers.

## 1. Store Leftovers Correctly

To extend the life of your leftovers, store them properly. Allow your food to cool to room temperature before refrigerating to avoid bacterial growth. Once cooled, place the leftovers in airtight containers to keep them fresh and prevent contamination. Label the containers with the date so you can track when they were made.

If you don't plan to eat the leftovers within a few days, freezing them is an excellent option. Use freezer-safe containers or bags, and consider portioning out meals into single servings for easy reheating. Always leave a bit of room in the container for expansion as the food freezes.

## 2. Reheat Properly

When reheating leftovers, it's important to do so safely to preserve flavor and texture. Avoid reheating multiple times, as this can degrade the food's quality and lead to uneven heating. Reheat your leftovers to an internal temperature of 165°F (74°C) for safe consumption.

Soups, stews, and sauces can be reheated on the stovetop or in the microwave. If the consistency has thickened, add a little broth or water to adjust. For meats, reheating in the oven or stovetop with some oil or broth helps retain moisture and tenderness.

3. Repurpose Leftovers into New Dishes

Leftovers don't have to be boring. With a little creativity, you can repurpose them into new and exciting meals. For example:

Soups and stews: Leftover soup can be used as a pasta sauce or filling for a savory casserole.

Meats: Leftover meats such as chicken, pork, or beef can be turned into tacos, sandwiches, or salads.

Vegetables: Leftover roasted vegetables make a great addition to a frittata, pasta dish, or grain bowl.

Repurposing leftovers not only reduces food waste but also provides an opportunity to experiment with new flavors and meals.

4. Freeze for Later

If you have more leftovers than you can eat in a few days, freezing is a great solution. Most slow-cooked meals freeze well, and you can enjoy them later. Just make sure the food is completely cooled before freezing, and use freezer-safe containers or bags. Label your frozen meals with the date and contents for easy identification.

Avoid freezing dairy-based sauces, as they can separate when reheated. However, many slow-cooked dishes, such as soups, stews, and casseroles, actually taste even better after freezing because the flavors continue to develop.

5. Add a Fresh Twist

Even if your leftovers are a few days old, you can make them feel like a new dish by adding fresh ingredients. A squeeze of citrus, fresh herbs, or a dollop of yogurt or sour cream can reinvigorate your leftovers. Small touches like a sprinkle of cheese, a handful of greens, or a drizzle of olive oil can transform your leftover meal into something fresh and exciting.

# Appendix

This appendix serves as a practical reference to help you get the best results from your slow cooker and the recipes in this book. It includes essential measurement conversions, ingredient substitutions, troubleshooting tips, and food safety guidelines to ensure your cooking experience is smooth, efficient, and enjoyable.

1. Measurement Conversions

Understanding measurements is key to achieving the right balance of flavors and textures. Below are common conversions for liquid, weight, and dry ingredients.

- Liquid Measurements
- 1 teaspoon = 5 milliliters
- 1 tablespoon = 15 milliliters
- 1 cup = 240 milliliters
- 1 pint = 2 cups (480 milliliters)
- 1 quart = 4 cups (960 milliliters)
- 1 liter = 4.2 cups
- 1 gallon = 16 cups (3.8 liters)
- Weight Conversions
- 1 ounce = 28 grams
- 1 pound = 16 ounces (454 grams)

- 1 kilogram = 2.2 pounds
- Dry Ingredient Measurements
- 1 tablespoon = 3 teaspoons
- 1/4 cup = 4 tablespoons
- 1/3 cup = 5 tablespoons + 1 teaspoon
- 1/2 cup = 8 tablespoons
- 1 cup = 16 tablespoons
  - ○

2. Ingredient Substitutions

If you find yourself missing an ingredient, these substitutions can help maintain the integrity of your dish without compromising flavor or texture.

Heavy cream → Full-fat coconut milk or a mixture of milk and butter (¾ cup milk + ¼ cup melted butter)

Sour cream → Plain Greek yogurt or buttermilk

Butter → Coconut oil or olive oil (for cooking)

Brown sugar → White sugar + molasses (1 cup sugar + 1 tablespoon molasses)

Buttermilk → 1 cup milk + 1 tablespoon lemon juice or vinegar (let sit for 5 minutes)

Fresh herbs → 1 teaspoon dried herbs for every 1 tablespoon fresh herbs

Garlic cloves → ¼ teaspoon garlic powder per clove

## 3. Slow Cooker Troubleshooting

Even with precise recipes, slow cooking can sometimes require adjustments. Here are solutions to common issues you may encounter:

If the food is cooking too fast or too slow:

Some modern slow cookers run hotter than older models. If food is cooking too quickly, reduce the heat or shorten the cooking time.

If the food is undercooked, ensure the lid remains closed as much as possible, and check that the slow cooker is at least half full for even heating.

If the dish is too watery or thin:

Slow cookers trap moisture, which can lead to overly thin soups or stews. To thicken your dish:

Remove the lid for the last 30 minutes of cooking to allow some liquid to evaporate.

Stir in a cornstarch slurry (1 tablespoon cornstarch mixed with 2 tablespoons water).

Add ingredients that naturally absorb liquid, such as rice, lentils, or potatoes.

If the flavors aren't strong enough:

Slow cooking can mellow flavors. To enhance the taste:

Adjust seasoning towards the end of cooking.

Add a splash of acid (lemon juice, vinegar) or fresh herbs before serving for brightness.

## 4. Food Safety Guidelines

Proper food handling ensures that your meals remain safe and delicious. Follow these key guidelines:

Never place frozen meat directly into the slow cooker. Always thaw meat in the refrigerator beforehand to prevent uneven cooking.

Store leftovers properly. Refrigerate cooked food in airtight containers within two hours of cooking and consume within three to four days.

Reheat leftovers thoroughly. Ensure food reaches an internal temperature of 165°F (74°C) before serving.

Do not overfill the slow cooker. For best results, fill it between half and two-thirds full.

Final Thoughts

Using a slow cooker is one of the easiest ways to create delicious, home-cooked meals with minimal effort. With the right techniques, high-quality ingredients, and an understanding of slow cooking principles, you can enjoy flavorful, perfectly portioned meals every time. This cookbook was designed to make cooking simple, enjoyable, and efficient—without excess portions of food waste.

Thank you for choosing this book as your guide to slow cooking. May your kitchen always be filled with warmth, rich aromas, and satisfying meals. Happy cooking!

We will like to hear from you soon, feedback about this book will make this book more visible to more customers. Thank you so much.

# BONUS

3-Week Slow Cooker Meal Plan

Week 1

Day 1

Breakfast: Slow Cooker Overnight Apple Cinnamon Steel-Cut Oats
Lunch: Slow Cooker Lentil Soup with Sweet Potato and Coconut Milk
Dinner: Slow Cooker Coq au Vin for Two

Day 2

Breakfast: Slow Cooker Banana Bread Oatmeal
Lunch: Slow Cooker Pineapple Chicken with Coconut Rice
Dinner: Slow Cooker Moroccan Lamb with Apricots and Almonds

Day 3

Breakfast: Slow Cooker Mixed Berry Compote with Greek Yogurt
Lunch: Slow Cooker Vegetarian Chili with Apples and Butternut Squash
Dinner: Slow Cooker Beef Bourguignon

Day 4

Breakfast: Slow Cooker Pumpkin Pie Oatmeal
Lunch: Slow Cooker Balsamic Glazed Brussels Sprouts with Cranberries and Pecans
Dinner: Slow Cooker Pork Tenderloin with Fig and Port Sauce

Day 5

Breakfast: Slow Cooker Breakfast Quinoa with Fruit and Nuts
Lunch: Slow Cooker Maple-Glazed Salmon with Quinoa
Dinner: Slow Cooker Duck Confit with Cherry Sauce

Day 6

Breakfast: Slow Cooker Chocolate Peanut Butter Fudge
Lunch: Slow Cooker Honey Garlic Chicken with Sweet Potatoes
Dinner: Slow Cooker Halibut with Mango Salsa

Day 7

Breakfast: Slow Cooker Dulce de Leche (Caramel)
Lunch: Slow Cooker Coconut Curry Lentil Soup
Dinner: Slow Cooker Chicken with Preserved Lemons and Olives

Week 2
Day 8

Breakfast: Slow Cooker Rice Pudding
Lunch: Slow Cooker Lemon Herb Tilapia with Garlic Butter Green Beans
Dinner: Slow Cooker Vegetarian Tagine with Dates and Almonds

Day 9

Breakfast: Slow Cooker Overnight Apple Cinnamon Steel-Cut Oats
Lunch: Slow Cooker Turkey Meatballs with Cranberry Sauce
Dinner: Slow Cooker Coq au Vin for Two

Day 10

Breakfast: Slow Cooker Pumpkin Pie Oatmeal

Lunch: Slow Cooker Pineapple Chicken with Coconut Rice
Dinner: Slow Cooker Moroccan Lamb with Apricots and Almonds

Day 11

Breakfast: Slow Cooker Banana Bread Oatmeal
Lunch: Slow Cooker Lentil Soup with Sweet Potato and Coconut Milk
Dinner: Slow Cooker Beef Bourguignon

Day 12

Breakfast: Slow Cooker Mixed Berry Compote with Greek Yogurt
Lunch: Slow Cooker Vegetarian Chili with Apples and Butternut Squash
Dinner: Slow Cooker Duck Confit with Cherry Sauce

Day 13

Breakfast: Slow Cooker Chocolate Peanut Butter Fudge
Lunch: Slow Cooker Balsamic Glazed Brussels Sprouts with Cranberries and Pecans
Dinner: Slow Cooker Pork Tenderloin with Fig and Port Sauce

Day 14

Breakfast: Slow Cooker Breakfast Quinoa with Fruit and Nuts
Lunch: Slow Cooker Maple-Glazed Salmon with Quinoa
Dinner: Slow Cooker Halibut with Mango Salsa
Week 3

Day 15

Breakfast: Slow Cooker Rice Pudding
Lunch: Slow Cooker Honey Garlic Chicken with Sweet Potatoes
Dinner: Slow Cooker Chicken with Preserved Lemons and Olives

Day 16

Breakfast: Slow Cooker Pumpkin Pie Oatmeal
Lunch: Slow Cooker Lemon Herb Tilapia with Garlic Butter Green Beans
Dinner: Slow Cooker Vegetarian Tagine with Dates and Almonds

Day 17

Breakfast: Slow Cooker Banana Bread Oatmeal
Lunch: Slow Cooker Coconut Curry Lentil Soup

Dinner: Slow Cooker Beef Bourguignon

Day 18

Breakfast: Slow Cooker Dulce de Leche (Caramel)
Lunch: Slow Cooker Turkey Meatballs with Cranberry Sauce
Dinner: Slow Cooker Moroccan Lamb with Apricots and Almonds

Day 19

Breakfast: Slow Cooker Mixed Berry Compote with Greek Yogurt
Lunch: Slow Cooker Lentil Soup with Sweet Potato and Coconut Milk
Dinner: Slow Cooker Duck Confit with Cherry Sauce

Day 20

Breakfast: Slow Cooker Chocolate Peanut Butter Fudge
Lunch: Slow Cooker Pineapple Chicken with Coconut Rice
Dinner: Slow Cooker Pork Tenderloin with Fig and Port Sauce

Day 21

Breakfast: Slow Cooker Breakfast Quinoa with Fruit and Nuts
Lunch: Slow Cooker Balsamic Glazed Brussels Sprouts with Cranberries and Pecans

Dinner: Slow Cooker Halibut with Mango Salsa

---

Made in the USA
Monee, IL
14 April 2025

15709118R00077